SAVED BY
THE BELL

RON NEEDLE

To Joyce + Frank,

Sincere Best Wishes

Ron Needle

21-01-16

TAIL END PUBLICATIONS

© Ron Needle 2006

Second impression 2015

ISBN   978-0-9554088-0-9

Published by:
Tail End Publications
66 High Street
Langford
Biggleswade
Bedfordshire
SG18 9RU

A CIP catalogue record of this book
can be obtained from the British Library.

Book designed by Michael Walsh at The Better Book Company •
5 Lime Close • Chichester • West Sussex • PO19 6SW

Printed by ImprintDigital.net • Seychelles Farm • Upton Pyne •
Exeter • Devon • EX5 5HY

Sergeant Ron Needle

1945

CONTENTS

I DEDICATE MY STORY EQUALLY TO:

RUBY, REG, ANDRÉ, YVETTE

AND

THE VILLAGERS OF MÉLIGNY-LE-GRAND

Ruby and Reg Mann, my sister and brother-in-law, proposed and organised our first trip to Méligny and it was Ruby who wrote a short piece that inspired me to write this story. Without their encouragement and help it is possible that I may never have returned to find the village. I truly believe that the humanity shown by the villagers of Méligny-le-Grand to Harry Stunnell and I on that fateful day of 8th January, 1945, is worthy of far more than just my dedication.

I would like to thank my wife Sylvia for showing great patience and support as I worked on this story, as well as my eldest daughter Sue, her husband Aggy, and Maria my youngest daughter. Special thanks go to all those involved in my rescue and/or first reunion:

My sister Gladys, Michael Dryden, André and Yvette Fromont and all their family, Henri Guérin the Mayor of Méligny, Colette Presson and her late husband Guy, the late Madam Bouchot, her son René along with his wife Madeleine and his two sisters.

Further thanks go to Claude and Nicole Amiot, Michel and Louise Giroux, Anne Marie Vauthier and her late husband Jean along with all their family, Jean and Louise Hasselwander, Dominique Wagner the new Mayor of Méligny-le-Grand, and all the villagers who were involved in saving the lives of Harry and me. Thanks also go to the late Des Richards and Alan Strudwick and last, but not least, Dr. Tom J. Renouf M.M. and Katherine his wife – they all helped in our many visits to Méligny.

During the writing of this book Maria and her partner Stuart have presented us with our latest grandson Joe who has given us great joy in our old age. (Stuart Ford is a fine musician - being an excellent guitarist is one of his many strengths!) Our other grandchildren Samantha by Renny and Nita; Sally, Sophia and Stefanos by Sue and Aggy; and Jude by Renny and Karen, are all very special to me. **"I love my grandchildren. I should have had them first!"** Whilst writing this story Samantha has given us three great-grandchildren Ella, Moya and Macoi. Prior to the reprint of this book Sally and her husband Richard have presented me with a further three great-grandchildren Amelie-Rose, Ruby and Maia. Sadly I have lost some of my siblings during this period, my fellow survivor Harry, as well as my beloved wife Sylvia.

Throughout the time of writing I have seen my handwritten notes transformed into a well presented story through the efforts of Sue and her husband Aggy.

I thank God for them all.

106 Squadron
Royal Air Force

Requiem for a Rear Gunner

*My brief sweet life is over,
my eyes no longer see,*

*No summer walks ~ no Christmas Trees ~
No Pretty girls for me,*

*I've got the chop, I've had it,
my nightly ops are done,*

*Yet in another hundred years,
I'll still be twenty-one.*

1

The Start of the Mission

Lancaster Bomber
Courtesy of the Imperial War Museum LH 12345

The date was June 20, 1986. It was a warm, pleasant, sunny Wednesday afternoon when we arrived at the Belle View Hotel not far from Calais. My wife Sylvia, sisters Ruby and Gladys, and brother-in-law Reg, were sitting with me at a garden table at the front of the hotel when a coach arrived. Forty young boys and girls alighted escorted by four women. The coach continued on in the direction of the village. To my surprise the women who had sat at a table not far from us began speaking in English. "Teachers" I imagined "bringing children aged about eleven to twelve on a French speaking holiday."

Dinner we were told would be at 1930 hrs. I was a little disappointed because I wanted to watch the England v Paraguay match at 2000 hrs. Never mind, we were all feeling elated at being in France – I could possibly see the last half hour of the match afterwards. The meal itself was fun, although none of us could speak French and we were unable to make the lovely young French waitress understand that we wanted a sweet wine with our meal. Reg got up from his chair and walked over to one of the English women sitting at another dining table and asked if she could explain to the waitress for us. "Of course," she said, "I would be happy to." We were all amused at the way the dialogue went together with the facial expressions involved. Eventually we were served a very palatable wine and took our time enjoying the meal. After we had drunk our coffee I asked to be excused so I could go into the lounge and watch the end of the football match. The others decided to go for a walk. I noticed the school party had also finished their meal and the pupils had gone to play on the large lawns situated at the rear of the hotel.

"Aren't I lucky?" I thought as I walked into the lounge. The TV was tuned to the channel covering the match and England was winning one nil. I sat down to enjoy the remaining twenty minutes. The Englishwoman who had translated for us looked at me and asked if we were on holiday. I decided to tell her the truth – we weren't really on holiday, more of a mission. I gave her the brief details and she responded warmly asking if I would please tell this story to the children. "Yes," I said, though I must admit that whilst eating my meal I wondered if the children would really like to hear the story of my mission. She then introduced me to her colleagues. Her name was Mrs. P. Smith, the Group Leader from Uplands Primary School, Sandhurst in Surrey.

Before the match had ended she informed me that the children were ready when I was. My mind wasn't really on the match, particularly as England had scored a second goal, so I went outside where the children were waiting with a chair ready for me. I took a deep breath, sat down and said – "Well boys and girls," ...

Forty-one years ago at the age of 19 I was a Rear Gunner in a Lancaster Bomber of 106 Squadron, No. 5 Group, based at Metheringham near Lincoln. The Squadron was taking part in a bombing mission, my twelfth, and the second to Munich. Flight plans were much as before. We were given the height and course for the bombing run along with the basic rule of

2

avoiding collisions over the target – or at least that was what we thought. As I recall it was a moonlit night when we started and very cold. It was winter, January 7, 1945, to be exact.

No sign of enemy fighters as we started the bombing run and, not being a hero, I felt relieved when Jock, our bomb aimer, said, "Bombs away." "Good," I thought, "now we can go home." Suddenly the plane went out of control. I didn't even have time to think what had happened – self-survival was

Author aged nineteen

all that mattered. I tried to bail out of my turret exit but couldn't as the G force was too great. After what seemed an eternity the plane once again flew on a level course. The pilot Jimmy, a Scot like Jock, had managed with God's help to regain control. He called us up on the intercom to say another Lancaster had somehow flown back into the main stream of bombers. We had nearly collided but with great skill and quick reflexes Jimmy had averted the crash. As the planes passed each other we were caught in his slipstream and could have been turned over. Thank God for a good pilot. In the confusion, however, the bomb hatch had been ditched and icy cold air was sweeping into the aircraft. We had to try and reach a height of 16,000 ft. to get over the Alps on our way home. The Skipper asked me to vacate my turret and pass my gloves down to the Navigator who needed them more than I did. He was the one we relied on to plot our course. I then sat at the rear of the plane and plugged in my intercom.

With our damaged plane, the Skipper decided to make for an emergency aerodrome near Paris. Once across the front line out of Germany the plane reduced height – I supposed to try and get us a little warmer. Some time afterwards I heard the Skipper ask the Mid-Upper-Gunner if he could see the 'deck' yet. With no sign of panic he said, "Yes Skipper, it's right below us." "It can't be," was the reply; "we're at 4,000 ft., safety height for the area." The altimeter must have gone haywire over the target giving us a false reading of our height. Within seconds I felt myself being flung forward out of my seat. We had crashed into a forest. The time was about 2000 hrs.

How long afterwards, I didn't know, but I found myself upright with the harness supporting me. It had somehow got caught up on part of the fuselage structure. This had undoubtedly saved my life.

The inside of the plane was on fire with the ammunition exploding as it lay on the conveyor rack. "I must get out" I thought and immediately pressed the harness release button and dropped to the floor. My right shoulder was dislocated and my right ankle and lower leg were very painful – I couldn't stand.

What happened to me next was impossible. Anyone who has flown in a Lancaster will know how difficult it was to open or shut the rear door. This was due to the large lever needed to ensure the door was kept shut. Was it really my hand that touched the lever and made the door open? I somehow raised myself and crawled out of the aircraft. As I lay propped up against a tree I thought of the life I'd lived, not once believing that I was going to die ...'

2

Early Memories

My family lived at 151 St. Vincent Street, Ladywood, Birmingham 16. It was a 'back to back' house and we lived at the front. The ground floor comprised a small living room kept warm by a back loaded open fire range with a fire guard placed round the front to prevent anyone falling onto the open fire. The kitchen was at the rear of the house, a poky little place, which contained the cooking stove. A door at the side led to an entry shared with our front next door neighbour. The entry led to the yard at the rear. On the first floor was a small bedroom where my mother and father slept. The second floor, that we called an "attic," contained two beds. A cellar under the living room was used to store coal. That was it!

To the left of us was another covered entry situated under the first floor bedroom. This entry allowed access to the four

Mom, Dad and siblings

sets of people who lived at the back. In the back yard were two communal toilets and each house carried its own 'lav' seat and toilet paper, normally newspaper torn into squares and held together by an S hook or bent nail. Funny but I can't ever remember the toilets being frozen. The water pipes were lagged with coarse brown cloth wrapped round them.

I remember very well the Brewhouses, as we called them, small buildings provided to do the washing. The neighbours also had to share the two Brewhouses each containing a large built-in sink and boiler with space underneath to build a fire. When I was a little older I used to light the fire and put the water in the boiler ready for my mother to do the washing. Washing was a full day's work then – no washing machine, spin or tumble dryers! If it was a fine day the washing lines virtually covered the yard, but what problems on rainy days! No wonder boys wore their shirts, socks and underpants for nearly a week! Same for the girls, no more than one change of knickers a week! A mangle was used to remove excess water from the clothes and consisted of two rollers about six inches in diameter with a big wheel at the side. One person would turn the big wheel whilst another would feed the clothes through the rollers, taking great care not to get their fingers trapped. There were accidents, of course, often resulting in mangled fingers. Each tenant had a specified day and time to do the washing. If that day was missed one would have to wait till the following week.

One memory has always remained with me about these yards – the broken bottle pieces set in cement along each dividing yard wall. This would not be allowed today and rightly so.

At the back of our house lived a widow. I can't remember her name but I was told she helped my mother when she was in labour with me. As she was Irish and I was born on St. Patrick's Day she persuaded my parents to give me a second Christian name "Desmond."

My father's name was Edward. He was a truly wonderful man. He worked as a Sorter at the main Post Office. To keep us reasonably well fed and dressed he would work long hours, particularly at Christmas. He became President of the Post Office Union and later in life he attended Labour Conferences. He was well respected by his supervisors who came to see him at home many years later after he had retired through ill health. Dad was born in 1895 and served in the First World War with the Royal Warwickshire Regiment. Unfortunately he was gassed at the Battle of the Somme and forever afterwards suffered with bronchitis which eventually led to his death at the age of 65. My father was very wise, always saying "life is sweet and whatever it holds for you make the most of it." I know that Dad was respected because as a Union Official he would fight tooth and nail if he believed that a colleague had been wronged.

As a teenager I believed the saying "Hard work never killed anyone" but later in life I realised that the saying was a myth.

My mother, who was seven years younger than my father, was born "Ellen Spears" but had her family and friends call her "Nell". On rare occasions at house parties when dad had a drink of beer, he would sing "Nellie Dean". Mum had two brothers and six sisters. They were a very close family. I was one of eleven children, the fourth eldest. At one time there were ten of us aged fourteen and under, and I was born on 17th March, 1925.

Dad was one of five children and was born at Balsall Common near Solihull. In his younger days he acted as a Drover taking cattle to the market in Birmingham – a long walk there and back. His father, my grandfather, and his housekeeper moved to Osler Street near Edgbaston Reservoir. Mum's mother and father lived directly opposite us. Grandma Spears was very gentle and would welcome us into her house and give us mugs of tea and pieces of toast on a Saturday. Grandad Spears was a character but he used to get drunk and sometimes hit my grandmother. On one occasion someone fetched my Uncle

Harry Spears who lived only a few doors away. Uncle Harry, to save his mother from harm, hit his father and knocked him down. My grandmother immediately hit her son saying he shouldn't have hit his father! I remember granddad mellowed with age and became much more relaxed and reasonable.

3

School Life

Recollections of my early childhood begin with going to school when I was five years old. I went to St. Barnabas School in Ladywood Road opposite the Children's Hospital. Being conditioned by my father's saying "make the most of life" I did, and in the main I enjoyed school. My favourite subjects were Maths, Reading and Writing. I wasn't too keen on History or Geography, but I later regretted this as they were two subjects in which I became very interested. I didn't realise at the time how important they were.

The teachers were very strict and most pupils, including me, had "six of the best" – the hands tingled but I never cried. I accepted that this caning was part of school life and I never complained. I must have been naughty. On one occasion, however, another boy in my class was naughty and the lady teacher asked me to go and borrow the cane from a teacher by the name of Mr. Cooper. In front of his class he decided to do the job for her. He gave me "six of the best". He thought the caning was for me and would not listen to my protestations. What a performance afterwards when I returned to my class and reported to my teacher what had happened. She immediately took me back into Mr. Cooper's room and really told him off in front of the whole class.

One of the main differences in schools between the 1930s and today was the relatively small amount of bullying that went on in my day. Nearly each class I was in had a boy called "Cock-of-the-class" – the tough boy who would fight anyone. He would not start a fight but any bully would get his come-uppance. The Cock-of-the-class was the "Good Guy," not the "Baddy". It is true we used to have fights in the playground, but there were only ever two involved, not like today where gang fights are common. The "bully" was the exception, not the norm. Then most children accepted discipline and punishment. Perhaps these helped one to have respect, not only for others, but also for oneself!

Young children of today are very similar to those in my day. The difference is in the reaction of the parents. Some children whinge and shed a few tears to get their own way but in my day most parents responded by saying "If you don't stop blarting (crying) I'll give you something to cry for." Invariably the crying would cease.

One of the nice things about school was having free milk and also having school parties.

At the rear of our house was a girl who was younger than me, her name was Iris. I was given the task of taking her to her first day at school. I suppose she became my first girlfriend because she was the first girl I kissed – mind you the location was strange. It was in the covered entry at the side of our houses and there was no light, it was pitch black!

My life as a child was, in the main, very happy and contented. I can honestly say that I was never hungry, we always had something to eat at main meal times – porridge and toast for breakfast, a cooked meal at midday and jam with bread and butter for tea. Sunday was always a treat with a sweet after our dinner (we called it pudding).

When dad worked nights he would come home, accompanied by our cat, and get our breakfast. The cat used to wait for him by the canal gate about 200 yards from our house. I used to think that the cat was just waiting for dad out of affection. I have since learned that cats go to anyone who will feed them! Our cat knew that dad, on reaching home, would feed him – he wasn't so daft.

One of our favourite pastimes was doing jigsaw puzzles. We all agreed that the most difficult was of an Indian Chief with a flowing headdress made of feathers. After it was completed, and it must have taken six to seven weeks, we turned the completed puzzle over on its back and numbered every piece! When the weather was fine we played outdoors with stilts – long poles with a block of wood about 18 inches from the ground. With our feet on the blocks and the top of the poles under our arms we used to see how far we could walk. We also played Tip Cat with a piece of wood similar to a cricket ball but tapered at each end. With another piece of wood held in either hand we would hit the end of the tip causing it to jump in the air. You could either hit it whilst in the air to see how far it would go, or see how many times you could keep hitting it without it falling to the ground. Playing marbles and five stones was also fun, but if we hadn't any marbles we used to use beer bottle tops and flick them to see who's landed nearest the wall.

Often we went to the park to play on the roundabout or swings; at other times we would play cricket or football. Of course sometimes we were naughty and played tricks on the neighbours. On one occasion I was standing outside our house when one of my brothers ran up the entry past me. He was closely followed by an irate lady neighbour who, upon seeing me, said "I've got you," and slapped my face. She had mistaken me for my brother. He had tied a piece of rope to two door knockers and then knocked on both doors. Somehow she had managed to break the rope.

Most of us lads learned to swim in the canal nearby. The water was filthy, you couldn't see six inches below the surface never mind the bottom! When I was about ten years old I was playing along the canal with some other lads when I decided to jump into an empty barge moored along the towpath. What I didn't know was that the barge was full of water. I managed to reach the cabin soaking wet and afraid to go home. Meanwhile two of the lads with us ran to my home and told my mum I was drowning. She dashed down to the canal and I knew she was pleased to see me alive. However, that didn't stop her grabbing my ear and escorting me home where I was dried out and sent to bed for my punishment. Yes we did have the cane but very rarely from our parents. There was a saying "Spare the rod and spoil the child." Whenever I had the cane I knew that I deserved it. I never thought less of my parents, in fact the older I became the more I respected them.

Bonfire night was good fun. The neighbours would get together and provide baked potatoes, sausages and chestnuts and, of course, loads of fireworks. We lads used to collect branches and anything that would burn. We used to go miles to collect branches from what we called the "posh houses" in Edgbaston.

I used to enjoy the occasions when the roads or streets were dug up and there was a night-watchman on duty. He had a hut where he used to sit and rest and also shelter in the bad weather. What I liked best was the coke brazier he had to keep warm. He would allow us to keep him company and tell us tales of his childhood. Nothing smelled better than when he cooked his breakfast of eggs and bacon on a shovel held over the fire. What happy memories most of us have!

Coronation Jubilee Day in 1935 was a day to remember. All the neighbours in the street joined forces to celebrate. Streets were closed to the little traffic that we did have in those days. Trestle tables were erected in the streets and everyone brought their own chairs. Cakes, jelly, blancmange, nice sandwiches, minerals and cups of tea were provided. Truly I don't know who helped to pay for the food, but it was a day to remember. One of the things I especially remember was the R101 Zeppelin flying over Birmingham.

My mother would send one of us to the chemist to buy a pennyworth of curry powder to flavour the gravy when we had rabbit. My brothers, sisters and I would argue about who should have the kidney. This was one of my favourite meals. We also used to argue about having the skin of the rice pudding because there was never enough to go round. Mum and dad were very fair, there were no favourites.

The baker used to deliver the bread on a horse and cart. Every Friday we all had one penny to spend. Nearly always we bought chocolates or sweets. Sometimes we would hire a bicycle from a man who kept "Bicycles for Hire". One penny for half an hour, or was it an hour? When dad was at home he taught us all how to play chess, draughts and cards – whist, solo and crib. We were never bored, making our own amusements.

In the 1930s there was a local newspaper called the "Gazette." One day a man knocked on our door and introduced himself as Mr. E. from the "Gazette". He said that if we had a copy of that morning's paper he would give my mum a ten shilling note. My mother was cute enough to say "Hang on, it's upstairs." In the kitchen she got my eldest brother, Ted, to nip out of the back door and rush to buy the paper from the newsagents only a few doors down the road. My mother got the ten shilling note – what a windfall in those days!

If we were lucky enough to be given an extra penny we would go the local picture house called the "Lyric" nicknamed "the Lousy House" because one could so easily catch fleas there. There were no seats, just long benches with no back rest. Like I say, "how times have changed." I well remember the male usher periodically going down each aisle with a scent spray. To be honest I have never had a good sense of smell. Perhaps I have been fortunate! I used to like, and still do, the Cowboy and Indian films. Tom Mix was my favourite. When someone asked what was my favourite film I would say "Tom Mix in Cement". I've always enjoyed a play on words.

Birthdays were always a treat, extra penny and a little present. My mother's next youngest sister Auntie Floss thought a lot of our mum. She was married to Uncle Bill and they were well off. Even in the late 30s they owned or were buying a house on Hay Barnes Road, Small Heath. We children had a lot to thank our Auntie Floss and Uncle Bill for. They always bought us a present on our birthdays, and Christmas wouldn't have been the same without the little presents they bought us. Auntie Floss allowed us to visit her home, as indeed did my other aunts. Auntie Floss would make us very welcome, but she wouldn't stand any nonsense, and would correct us if we misbehaved.

She taught me to accept discipline and punishment when it was deserved. How pleased I was that in my 60s I was able to tell Auntie Floss and Dorothy, my cousin, how very fortunate we were to have Aunty Floss and Uncle Bill in our lives.

All through my life I have been susceptible to the "flu". Some people say they have had the flu when I think it was just a heavy cold. My bouts made me delirious and kept me in bed for four to five days. One Christmas period I was in bed when the Salvation Army began playing carols outside the house. In my state I was utterly confused and truly frightened by their playing. This jogs my memory to an incident that occurred when I was eleven years old after we had been playing "Rummy". The game must have been playing on my mind because that night at about 10 o'clock I must have been sleepwalking. I went down the stairs to be met by my father who said, "What do you want son?" This must have woken me and I replied "I'm looking for the seven of Diamonds!" Luckily this was the only time such an incident occurred.

4

Earning Money

Money was short and many people went to "Uncles," the Pawnshop, on a Monday and hopefully redeem whatever was pawned on a Friday when the wages were paid. Funny, I can't remember having many new clothes, more like "hand-me-downs" passed from an elder brother or sister to the next youngest. It was no problem, we all accepted this as a way of life.

Before I was 12 years old I used to run errands for neighbours in order to raise a few coppers to give mum. In the winter I would go to a bachelor's house to light his fire so that he would have a warm room to come home to.

In the summer there was always a fair at Edgbaston Reservoir. I worked for weeks on "Hoop La" stalls. I loved this because not only was I paid but I had a cooked dinner with 'afters' every day! The one attraction I remember most was where I helped the performer, a man born without arms with only little growths from his shoulders. He would climb a ladder to a platform about 25 to 30 feet high above a round tank about 10 feet wide. One of his assistants would light the flammable liquid on the surface of the tank and he would jump or dive into the flaming tank. On hitting the water the flames went out and water spilled over the sides. How brave I thought he was!

My eldest brother Ted worked in the evenings and all day Saturday at a hairdressers whilst Gordon, the next oldest to me, worked at a 'fruit and veg' shop – both shops were in Monument Road near to the 'Ivy Bush'. When Gordon came home on a Saturday everyone was waiting for him as he was allowed to bring home some fruit and veg that wouldn't last the weekend. My sister Elsie in the meantime had reached 14 years of age and had started working full-time – 48 hours was the normal working week. Our standard of living was much better now. Mum still had to be careful though because other brothers and sisters were arriving on the scene. At one time we were sleeping both at the top and the bottom of the bed!

In 1937 a most welcome change occurred in my life. Due to the overcrowding we were given a 'Parlour' type house (council, semi-detached) at 163 Merritts Brook Lane, Northfield. It was a 3-bedroom house with a front room downstairs, a bathroom and a living room, a front garden and a large back garden with a lawn and a vegetable patch at the rear. To this day I call Northfield "God's country." Moving to Northfield was obviously a new chapter in my life and one that helped me to realise that life for us was a progression – from being poor and living in the slums to living and eating well in a most enjoyable environment. I suppose I saw this as a stepping stone to keep bettering my life.

School was never a problem for me. Of course there were subjects I didn't enjoy but, in the main, I looked forward to going to school. Perhaps I was lucky that the main school in "Tinkers Farm Road" was full as that meant I attended one of the few classes that were held at the Chapel in Chatham Road next door to Northfield Baths where I received more personal attention. Our teacher was a Mr. Harrison and his words to us when we were about to leave at 14 years of age have remained with me forever: "Remember when you have money in your pocket and are tempted to gamble on the horses, picture the bookmakers with their big cars and fat cigars and think where their money came from – the suckers who gamble!" Mr. Harrison's second piece of advice was "If you read half of the newspaper and believe half of what you read you will be half right." Some things never change.

After a short time delivering newspapers to earn pocket money and help my mother, I worked in a pork butcher's shop on the main Bristol Road South (no. 820) – in the mornings before school, in the evenings after school and all day Saturday. I loved this job, particularly meeting all the different kinds of people. In the main it taught me that we are all different, but politeness was the main theme. In those days the customers were always right, even when they weren't! I used to help make pork sausages, faggots and pressed brawn. There was a saying that the only things wasted on a pig were the ear holes, nose holes and the one at the back! I didn't get off to a very good start though because on the first day I sat down in front of a huge coal fire and fell asleep. Rather than it resulting in my being chastised it seemed to amuse everyone. I didn't do it again! Christmas time was busy feathering, cleaning and preparing chickens, turkeys and grouse for the oven. I didn't like grouse because the feathers were difficult to remove. Occasionally one would drop links of sausages on the floor. Before going home I was able to pick up the sausages, dip them into a clean bucket of water, and put them back for sale. Late on a Saturday, in order to sell as much as we could, we used to cut the bacon up razor thin and arrange it giving the impression there was a lot for 4p – a lot of slices but not much bacon! Before closing we would scrub the blocks, sweep up and put a fresh supply of sawdust on the floor.

The back slang used by most butchers amused me, e.g. Kcab spelt backwards is 'Back'. It was a way of conversing without the customers understanding. As I loved this job, after I left school I worked there full time. My wages went up to – wait for it – ten shillings (nowadays 50p) per week! I honestly can't remember if I had to pay for the overalls or not.

I had been at work for six months and one day, and with everyone at home listening to the radio, it was announced by Prime Minister Neville Chamberlain, that War had been declared on Germany. The date was September 3rd 1939. At the age of 14, of course, I didn't really comprehend what War meant but I was soon to learn.

One Monday I was about half an hour late for work. I wasn't worried because I knew there wasn't much to do – at least that was what I thought. However, when I arrived the boss was there with the rest of the staff busily making a large consignment of pork sausages that I didn't know about. I suppose that was my first lesson that no-one is indispensable because the boss was so upset he sacked me immediately. I was in the wrong. I must have been 16 years old then, the year 1941.

5

Your Country Needs You!

Uncle Les, my mum's brother, was called up by the army. He was lost at sea en route to serving in Greece. My Auntie Doris' brother-in-law, also in the army, was killed at Dunkirk whilst waiting to be picked up on the beaches. I saw my first enemy aircraft one Wednesday afternoon whilst in the back garden at home. This was the day when the butchers closed at midday. Thinking back it was the moment when I decided that, if the War went on and I had to enlist, I wanted to fly.

It wasn't long before everyone had an Anderson Air Raid shelter given to them to erect in the back garden. The shelter consisted of corrugated sections of steel sheets about six feet high, six and a half feet long and four and a half feet wide, similar to a shed, but with no door, just an opening at the front

Anderson Shelter. A land mine fell a few yards away from this one – three inhabitants got away safely.
Courtesy of Imperial War Museum D5949

to enter. With the help of us lads my father dug about five feet below the surface of the garden and placed the soil on top. Steps were made for quick access. It was really formidable. For many years a lot of tenants used these shelters as garden sheds. In the War years most people became blasé and either ignored the sirens or hid under the table or stairs. Mind you, I don't believe we would have done this if we had lived in London which took the full brunt of the bombing night after night. I thought the Londoners were very brave indeed.

There were ration books for food, sugar and clothes and people queued for hours to purchase a cigarette.

To counteract the ugliness of war my eldest sister, two elder brothers and I learned to dance and five nights a week we went to the local Community Hall where lessons were given by professional dancers. It was great – a five piece dance band. I think the leader's name was Billy Donnelly and the MC a very big gentleman called Harry Flaherty. He organised the dances, even to the extent of having competitions! I thought this was good because I have always been competitive and wanted not only to improve but also to beat my brothers in the competitions.

Next door to the Community Hall lived a girl called Sylvia Valente, later to become my wife. At first she would have no cotter (nothing) to do with me. Perhaps this was because, when I worked in the pork butchers shop, her mother would send her there for a pork chop for her dad and a pound of sausages for the rest of the family! She truly was the girl of my dreams. She wore a black and white dress, the skirt pleated from the waist down mixed with black and white stripes. Most of us had permanent dancing partners. Some, of course, became engaged but others, like myself, had a partner where romantic attachments didn't take place – we were just good friends, but I still had eyes for Sylvia. Eventually Sylvia and I did get together and I vividly remember our first kiss. She must have thought I was awful! It was a pitch black night, no moon or street lights and I kissed her when I said "goodnight" to her at her garden gate. The kiss ended with a lip-smack! I was very embarrassed but so happy.

For months, on arriving home after the dance on a Saturday night, we three brothers would have a bit of supper and then play cards all through Saturday night and into Sunday afternoon. To be fair we only played for pennies because most of the games played needed skill as well as luck – games like Whist, Solo and Rummy. I never did like purely gambling games such as Brag or Pontoon. I not only hated losing money, I couldn't afford to. Sometimes we did argue but in the main whoever won gave back the coppers to the losers. As time went on Ted, my eldest brother, was "called up" by the RAF. He trained as a fitter maintaining aircraft. Gordon joined the Army, becoming a driver in the Royal Army Service Corps. Both served overseas but luckily they both came home unscathed.

After leaving Dainties the pork butchers I was given a job at Austin Aero, one of a number of shadow factories that sprang up at the beginning of the War. My first job was as an apprentice toolmaker, but this wasn't my forte, and the wages weren't much either. Later I was able to transfer to the Stirling Bomber assembly line, but little did I realise when I was drilling and riveting the fuselage section that the time would come when I would hate the name 'Stirling Bomber'. It was, in my opinion, one of the worst Bombers in the RAF. This Bomber was soon made obsolete and used for training air crew only.

Everyone was made redundant when production ceased and we were all told to report to the local Employment Office. During the War there was something called the E.W.O. – Essential Works Order. Everyone over seventeen had to work where they were told to. When I reported I was told that I would have to go down the mines. I didn't fancy this and when I objected I was told the alternative was to be called up by the Armed Forces. I retorted that I wished to be called up. The interviewer softened when I said this and, instead, sent me to a little firm by the name of Austers. They specialised in experimental work for the Air Ministry making gun turrets and bomb aimer compartments. One day the General Manager sent for me and said that now I was seventeen and a half I had to be registered for the Armed Forces. He told me that if I didn't volunteer he would be able to stop me being called up as the type of work we were doing was classed as a reserved occupation. I did tell him a lie when I said I wouldn't volunteer, giving the impression I would stay in the job. I wanted to fly and thought perhaps this was the chance I had been waiting for.

The day of my registering arrived and I had to report to the RAF recruiting office at Viceroy Flats in Bristol Street, Edgbaston. How proud I was when I passed my medical and introduction exam to be an Air Gunner. It was only years later that I realised how upset it made my mum and dad because they, more than me, understood how dangerous it would be.

6

The Royal Air Force

I was only 18 when, in September, 1943, I reported to the induction centre in St. John's Wood, London. Here we were kitted out before being transferred after a fortnight to a training camp in Bridlington, Yorkshire. We were to learn the theory of air gunnery – gunnery itself, and aircraft recognition, as well as the usual 'square bashing'. Ex-servicemen know it is very rare to get a good Flight Sergeant and a good Flight Officer. Our Flight Sergeant was a horrible man. I remember how one evening, after the day's training, we were waiting for his daily inspection. I was billeted with about twenty others in a house requisitioned by the War Office. A few of the other lads in the house had been in the RAF for some time. They had re-mustered volunteering for aircrew duties. When the Flight Sergeant was late they started to sing "Why are we waiting?" Suddenly the Flight Sergeant appeared. With a snarl he said, "I'll show you why you're waiting" – and he confined us to our rooms for the night. Afterwards the incident amused me. I still smile now when I think of it. At the time I felt a little scared of him, but he taught us to accept discipline.

Lancaster Bomber

I look back on our Officer with happier memories. He was a true gentleman, and I learnt from him that you don't need to have money to be one. My young aunt was getting married while I was at Bridlington. When I applied for a weekend pass to be at the wedding my application was turned down. Feeling very disappointed and rather low I went to bed very early and started to write a letter to my girl Sylvia. I looked up and, to my surprise, the Officer had entered the room. He said he realised how I felt and if I promised to be back by midnight on the Sunday I could have my weekend pass. I was elated. I was thrilled to go home and show everyone my uniform and, of course, the white flash on my peak cap which only air crew trainees were allowed to have. I also made sure I was back on time.

One other incident comes to mind. One of our lessons was attending the Air Force Commander's Parade. Walking through the streets of Bridlington I realised I had forgotten to pick up my cap. I was bare headed! I thought I would be court-marshalled, but of course I wasn't. However, I was the only one of hundreds on Parade who was wearing a steel helmet!

From Bridlington I was sent to a place called Stormy Downs near Pyle in Glamorgan. This was the start of the Flying and Air Gunnery practice. A plane, a Martinet, would tow a Drogue while an Anson aircraft with three Air Gunners would take turns firing at the Drogue. This part of the training was great, but I thought the pilots of the Martinets towing the Drogue were brave because sometimes the trainee Gunners didn't stop firing when the pilot altered course and the towing plane came into line with the Drogue. It was not uncommon for the Pilot of the towing aircraft to announce angrily on the radio, "I am towing this so-and-so thing, not pushing it!"

Also at the camp were a number of Canadians, most of whom loved to gamble playing cards. One of these entered the Inter Flight Boxing Competition – I do not think it is fair to mention his name although I remember it well. He was boxing against a very good English amateur who was making him look rather foolish. In the third and final round the Canadian suddenly unleashed a punch which caught his English opponent flush on the jaw. I had heard the expression 'pole-axed' before, but that was the one and only time I had ever seen it happen! Most boxers, when being knocked out, buckle at the knees before collapsing but this chap went backwards falling to the floor like a rigid pole. He was spark out but thankfully he fully recovered. I bet he wished he had thumped that Canadian when he had had the chance to in the first two rounds.

I mentioned the Canadians gambling because I saw this same chap losing to a Scotsman playing brag. The former offered to cut the cards for double or quits, though I feel sure he had no money left. He lost, but then pressurised his opponent to keep cutting the cards until he won and then he would not cut again – most unfair. This put me off gambling for ever.

When the course was completed we were asked to hand to the adjutant pairs of names of those who wanted to fly together, one to be a Mid-Upper-Gunner and the other the Rear Gunner. A Scotsman named Jim Morrison and I had become good friends and had given in our names as a pair.

After 14 days leave I had to report to an aerodrome at Bruntingthorpe, No 29 Operational Training Unit near Leicester. Here crews were made up and the training included cross country flights, flight engineering, practice bombing and air gunnery practice. I looked around for Jimmy, but no sign of him. Others, like me, couldn't find their partners either. The authorities had deliberately split us up. On reflection they were right, it taught us not to get too involved with friendships, though comradeship was very prevalent among the crews. The crew I teamed up with had as our pilot a very tall officer Flying Officer Hughes. The Navigator, Peter, came from Cornwall and the Bomb Aimer, Robert Dunlop, came from Edinburgh. They were Officers. Les, our Flight Engineer, came from Surbiton in Surrey and Billy Swift, our Mid Upper Gunner, came from St Helens near Liverpool.

I remember Billy from Stormy Downs. The CO was keen on boxing and we often had inter-flight bouts. Billy, being a 'pro' fighter, gave demonstration fights with the PT instructor. In the ring you would have thought they hated each other, the way they fought. As soon as the fight was over, however, they were the best of mates. Billy said he had sparred with Peter Kame, a champion, and he had broken Peter's nose whilst training for his world title fight. Within days, however, we lost Flying Officer Hughes who was posted to an active squadron. He replaced a pilot who went missing, presumed killed, while flying as an observer with another crew. Our replacement pilot was another Scot from Musselburgh near Edinburgh, Flight Sergeant Jimmy Scott. We learned later that F/O Hughes was awarded the DFC for bravery. We were all pleased for him.

Training here was almost complete. We only had to do one more night flight of circuits and bumps, but this was proving very difficult because of continuous bad weather. Leicester, not being far from Birmingham, made it easy for me to get home. Discipline did not appear so rigid now and I used to ring up and ask if we were flying. If not I stayed at home for another day. My parents were so proud the day I brought the crew home. We had a party. That was a night to remember.

One night I rang in to be told we would be flying at 0800 hrs the next morning. I well remember that night, I caught a late train to Leicester and was wearing my Best Blues and Shoes. The aerodrome was 12 miles away. I walked every step of the way with blisters on both feet. Being late I decided to make my way to the briefing room. When I arrived the instructor asked where the hell I had been. I said I had overslept. "What, in your Best Blues?" he retorted, then "Hurry up and get into your flying kit." It was only then that I realised that, apart from Jimmy, I was the only one present. Apparently the rest of the crew had been to Leicester the previous night and hadn't got back.

All the crew were put on a charge. The CO, Squadron Leader Kennedy, gave us all a rocket and the rest of the crew lost five days of privileges. As I had flown on the exercise he excused me. Wasn't I lucky? Was I? Read on – I went home again but, due to a delayed train, was late returning. On entering the Guard Room I learned with horror I had been reported AWOL. This time I was in front of the CO on my own. He decided to cancel our last training exercise and was sending the crew on leave pending a posting to the conversion unit. As for me, he gave me two days loss of privileges. The lads went on leave. I had to stay behind. Ironic, wasn't it?

Arriving at the Conversion Unit near Newark in Nottingham we carried out further training flights in Stirling Bombers. These were most cumbersome aircraft and were no longer being used for operational purposes.

The winter weather was still preventing flying every day. Hence a football match had been arranged between the Ground Staff and the Air Crew. Billy and I were playing alongside each other up front. One of the opposing ground staff was obviously a very good player but inclined to be rough. Two or three times he deliberately tripped Billy, then ran away smiling to himself. Eventually, feeling very aggrieved, Billy walked up to him and said very quietly but firmly "Pack it in." The man was about 5ft 10inches tall and about 13 stone whereas Billy was only 5ft 4ins and just over 10 stone.

Foolishly he tripped Billy up again – Billy picked himself up, walked to the big half back and, like a flash of lightning, threw out a left hand deliberately just missing the man's chin. He then cocked his right hand and said, "The next one won't miss you." Well the look on this man's face will remain with me always. His mouth opened wide and a strange look of surprise came to his face. He looked into Billy's cold blue eyes and then very sheepishly walked away. The lesson had been learned and he never came near Billy again. Over the years I have often thought of Billy and wondered how and what he was doing.

When real flying commenced an incident happened that I shall always remember. We were on a night training exercise in a Stirling Bomber doing practice bombing over Wainfleet Marshes near Skegness, as well as fighter affiliation using a cine camera. I was sitting in the rear turret having carried out my part of the exercise, and we then went on the practice bombing run. The night was very dark, no moon and very cloudy. Suddenly I felt myself being forced downwards on my seat. I looked up and saw the ground – "What the hell is going on?" I thought. I could not understand what was happening. After what seemed an eternity the plane flew on an even course, but vibrating very badly. The Skipper called up the control tower and asked permission for an emergency landing. Was I glad to get out onto solid earth! We had flown into the base of a huge cumulus cloud. This type of cloud contains currents of air so severe, I remember being told, that some light aircraft had been known to disintegrate after being sucked upwards. This was another occasion where I thanked God for having Jimmy as our Pilot. What strength he must have had to regain control.

After this incident our Navigator, Wireless Operator and Mid-Upper-Gunner were grounded. Replacements arrived the next day. We spent a few days at a Lancaster finishing school and were eventually posted to 106 Squadron at Metheringham near Lincoln at the end of October 1944.

At last the day arrived. I remember walking through the door of the billet I was to share with Harry our Wireless Operator, Les our Flight Engineer and Jack our Mid-Upper-Gunner. Other crew members were sitting round a table playing Monopoly. Harry commented, for something to say as an introduction, "Everyone seems flak happy round here." The reply from one of the players makes me smile every time I think of it – "You'd be bloody flak happy if you'd had flak up your arse."

The billet was very warm with a solid fire stove at each end – sheets on the bed too for the first time since enlisting. This was luxury living, but our part in Squadron training still had to take place. Two of the Lancasters we trained in were from the famous 617 Dam Busters Squadron led by

Wing Commander Guy Gibson VC that destroyed the Sorpe, Mohne and Eder Dams in May, 1943, thereby flooding the Ruhr valley and disrupting German industry. Prior to this raid, which forms such an important part of the history of Bomber Command, this gallant Officer commanded 106 Squadron, my squadron. Knowing this made me feel so proud. The planes themselves looked so strange – to enable them to carry the once famous bouncing bombs the sides of the bomb bays had been removed. They looked nothing like the elegant bombers the Lancasters were. Even today I still think that a Lancaster is a very beautiful aircraft. After five more training flights we were ready for our first operation. The date was to be November 15th, 1944.

November 15th 1944 – after a cooked meal of spam and chips – a luxury during the War – all the air crews assembled in the briefing room. The target was a synthetic oil plant in Harburg near Hamburg. Bomb load was 15,200 lb and the height over the target was to be 18,000 ft. We took off during the late afternoon – I felt so strange. The Group Captain and Ground Staff were waving us off. Over the North Sea flying towards Germany the sun was shining and I was rotating my turret, scouring the skies from port to starboard. Suddenly I felt as though someone had put a large bag over the plane. I lost visibility and it scared me. How tense I must have been, all that had happened was that we had entered cloud and I hadn't been expecting it! Over the target the anti aircraft fire (flak) didn't seem too bad, we did spot an unidentified aircraft but it did not attack us. We dropped our bombs and I was told the target area was being devastated. We Gunners never looked at the target area as bright lights affect night vision. It takes about 10 minutes for eyes to adjust to the dark.

The return journey was uneventful until we were about to land. To my horror two of our bombers collided over base and crashed. After landing we returned to the briefing room, made our reports and went to bed about two o'clock in the morning. I was glad the first raid was over. It had scared me but I felt I could cope now.

November 16th – this was the most vivid raid I ever went on. We were going on a daylight raid. The targets were transport and communications at Duren near Aix La Chapelle in France. At our briefing we were told the Germans had dug in and were holding up the allied advance. I believe the raid was carried out by the largest fleet of aircraft ever assembled and because of this we were given time of arrival, height and course over the target. Bomb load 13,000 lb, height 10,000 ft.

After taking off we flew outward over London. Was this to show the Londoners that we were having revenge for all they had suffered? The sky was full of planes. Once over France we found that we were early so we had to make a few dog legs, first flying to port then to starboard, eventually returning to our proper course. Nearing the target I remember looking up and seeing other Lancasters all around us. One in particular was worrying me. I was convinced that when he dropped his bombs they would hit us. To this day, I can never be sure if I was glad that when I looked up all I saw was a puff of smoke. He had been hit by flak and exploded.

Listening to the intercom I heard the voice of a man who became my hero – Group Captain Leonard Cheshire. He was the leader. Can anyone imagine a man being so brave? The sky was full of bombers and he was flying a Mosquito at roof top height directing operations, being shot at by all types of gun fire and also in danger of being hit by our bombs. He had arrived first over the target with a Pathfinder Squadron. They dropped different coloured flares and he stayed over the target area deciding which flares to use as bomb markers. Before we started our bombing run we could hear him directing operations – "First ones in to bomb the yellow flare with a two-second delay." When we started our run he instructed us to use a five-second delay.

Half an hour after leaving the target and well into Holland, we could still hear him directing the Operation. The target area must have been obliterated. What a man! I felt humbled and proud to be involved with such a man. I believe he must have given courage to everyone who flew on his missions including me. How anyone or anything could survive such an attack I do not know. The advance was held up for several more days, however. There must have been brave Germans as well.

November 21st – our third operational raid, another night on the Dortmund-Ems Canal at Ladbergen. Bomb load again 13,000 lb. Arriving over the target area cloud was dense and the skipper decided to come below the cloud and bomb from 3,000 ft. I remember the flak was only moderate when Jock called "Bombs away." Shortly after I heard explosions and the plane literally shook. "We've been hit," I thought. The explosions we heard were, in fact, our own bombs going off. We had caught our own blast. We were not in any danger, just fear of the unknown. In the excitement, however, the Navigator's maps and paperwork had become scattered. It took him some time before he could give the Skipper a course home. I remembered the Skipper becoming concerned, "Hurry up Navigator," he called, "we're heading towards the Ruhr," the most heavily defended part of Germany. Again I felt scared and very relieved when a course was given to take us home.

This type of raid was a regular for Bomber Command. Apparently after each raid on the canal "Jerry" conscripted hundreds of workers from German occupied countries to repair the damage. When our reconnaissance planes had spotted the repair work complete the RAF went out and bombed it again – it sounds so heartless but this was war!

November 22nd – our second longest flight; 9 hours 35 minutes. This time the target was the U-Boat pens near Trondheim in Norway. At the briefing we were told that we would have to take maximum petrol load. Even then some pilots may have felt that they would not have enough fuel to get home. If so, they could fly to neutral Sweden and be interned – some way to spend your War! As our instruments would be affected by the magnetic North Pole we had to use the coast line and stars for navigation.

When we took off, it was a filthy night – black as the ace of spades and pouring with rain. Heading towards Norway over the North Sea the Skipper attempted to climb over the clouds. Due to the weight of the bombs and the extra petrol we couldn't do this, so we had to fly under the clouds. I swear if I'd had a fishing rod I could have caught some fish, we seemed to be that low. I could see the white horses on the waves. Sometime afterwards we flew out of this bad weather and found ourselves in bright moonlight. What a sudden change! As we approached the target on our bombing run a message came over the radio. The mission was to be aborted; "Jerry" had put up a smoke screen. We were afraid our bombs might drop on the Norwegian village close by. Rather than risk killing innocent people, the raid was called off. The Skipper did a quick calculation and decided not to ditch our bombs. He did decide to make a detour, however, and make for Lossiemouth in Scotland, which was the nearest RAF aerodrome to Norway.

Flying over the mountains and fjords I thought "What a beautiful country, everything seems so peaceful in the moonlight." A lone German searchlight was scouring the sky. "Rear Gunner," the Skipper called out. "Would you like to have a go at it?" Sensing no danger, I replied "Yes Skipper." The plane started to reduce height as I prepared my guns and sight ready to fire. As if by magic, the sky suddenly became full of searchlights. Now we were the hunted. The Skipper said, "Let's get out of here," and we did.

Approaching Lossiemouth, I thought we were going to land in the sea. The Skipper had called up the control tower and been given permission to land. There was no problem though, the approach to the aerodrome was from the sea. When we landed we learned we only had a little petrol left. After breakfast and refuelling we headed home.

November 27th – a day, or should I say night, when I learned that I was not the only one who was scared. It was the way I found out that surprised me. We were called to the briefing room and, to my horror, the target was Berlin.

I honestly believe that was the first time I thought the odds were against me coming back. I was very afraid. Berlin was the most heavily defended target known. The percentage of planes lost bombing Berlin was frightening and the death toll very high. "Am I a coward?" I thought for when Berlin was mentioned a great cheer went up from the others. To my pleasant surprise we were called back to the briefing room to be told the raid was cancelled. The cheer that went up then was so much louder. Relief at not going made them react in a way they hadn't admitted before. I realised then that being scared was human and most people felt the same as me. This incident made me feel better.

November 30th. Our first raid to Munich. We were one of 287 bombers. Take off was 23.55 hours. Bomb load 7,555 lb and we had to fly at 16,990 ft, the target being so near to the Alps.

This was another raid I wasn't looking forward to. It would be a long flight, seven and a quarter hours to be exact. To combat the extreme cold I was wearing long johns and an electrically heated flying suit. You see, the Rear Gunner was exposed to the elements, no luxury like perspex to shield him. They say that even when perspex is thoroughly clean and polished it still cuts down normal vision by a third. This, of course, could be fatal when under attack by enemy fighters. The trouble was the electric suit wasn't working properly. There must have been a short circuit because my left side and leg were freezing and my right leg had started to burn me. Can you imagine how cold it had to be for teardrops to turn to ice before falling on my flying glove? Even so I think we were lucky not to see any enemy aircraft. Searchlights didn't pick us up and flak wasn't even noticeable.

After dropping the bombs we started our return journey crossing the Alps again, still in cloud. Now that we had used up nearly half the petrol the Skipper decided to fly above cloud. We had been climbing for some time when the Skipper called out "Rear Gunner, have we broken cloud yet?" "Not yet," was my reply. A little later the same question was asked and the same reply given. After the third time of asking, I don't know why, but I raised myself as high as I could and looked down. To my utter amazement the sky was clear, not a cloud in sight. What I thought was cloud was vapour trail. I felt such an idiot, if I hadn't looked down I reckon we could have broken the height flying record! We returned to the base and landed without further problems. After two or three more training trips – cross country, practice bombing and air to sea firing, we were briefed for our next raid, the sixth.

December 4th – the target: railway yards and junctions at Heilbronn. We were attempting to prevent or delay troops and munitions being transported to the ever-changing Western Front line. The bomb load was 11,000 lb, height 12,000 ft and take-off time 16.45 hours. Duration, six and three quarter hours. This was to be my most important operation yet – the day I think I came of age.

We reached the target area and started the bombing run whilst flying in cloud. Remember no fighters could find you if you were in cloud, particularly at night with no moon, and no radar like today. This did not stop me from rotating my turret and scouring even the murky clouds. I remembered my first raid when we flew into cloud and I had panicked momentarily. The bomb doors were still open when we broke cloud. Within seconds I spotted a JU88 enemy fighter hanging back on our starboard side. All my training was now to be tried out. "Enemy aircraft to starboard," I shouted over the intercom. "Prepare to dive starboard." This was the ploy used when attacked. By diving and turning into the enemy fighter's path it increased the gravitational pull on the enemy pilot. His guns were fixed to his wings and he had to train his plane onto the target. I remember opening fire but, in truth, I can't remember using my gun sight or working out distances and angle of fire but, horror of horrors, all four of my guns stopped firing – they had jammed. According to my training I could now free the jam by carrying out certain tasks. I did not attempt to do any.

34

All I could think of was to shout instructions to the pilot so he could carry out the evasive action. Six times the enemy fighter attacked us before breaking off and flying away.

We returned to base and landed. The crew and I quickly got out and scoured the aircraft for signs of damage. There was none. How great I felt when the Skipper, then the others slapped me on the back and said "Well done." Though afraid, I had still managed to do my job. What made us all feel on top of the world was when we saw the photographs we had taken of our bombs when they had gone off. The photos were so vivid, bombs exploding along the railway tracks bang on target. We were all elated.

December 6th – again the targets were railway junctions and flyovers at a place called Giesen in Germany. We carried 11 x 1000 lb bombs, flew in at 9,400 ft and were in the air for 6 hours 20 minutes. This time we were expecting enemy fighters. "Jerry" must have attached a great deal of importance to these types of targets because they were heavily defended. True to form we were attacked by another JU88 enemy night fighter – this time both before and after our bomb run. In fact during this raid I saw five enemy aircraft. I remember writing in my log book "no damage to us and no claims" whilst defending ourselves. We did bomb the target area though.

After this raid, our seventh, and because of the bad weather, we were given leave to return on December 20th. Travelling back to camp on the train the weather was still rotten with heavy snow. I was becoming more and more concerned because I knew I was going to be late. Hurrying through the gates I heard over the tannoy "Sergeant Needle please report to the briefing room" – this was repeated over and over again. With my heart in my mouth and almost breathless I reached the briefing room. The Flight Commander gave me an awful telling off saying I could have prevented a bomber joining an important raid. Luckily for me the raid was cancelled and I was not charged. I did realise the seriousness of the situation and I felt ashamed.

December 21st – my girlfriend Sylvia's birthday. I was thinking of her while relaxing in my "billet" when we were called once again to the briefing room. This was our longest flight, 10 hours and 5 minutes. For this operation our crew had been selected to join a group of twelve Pathfinders on a spoof raid. Our target was an airfield at Schneidemuhl. We carried 4 x 1000 lb bombs, 7 flares and a large quantity of aluminium foil known as "window."

Approaching the target we had our radio on so the enemy could hear us. We started to drop the foil to confuse their radar making them think we were a large force of bombers. We would then drop our flares, fly around again and drop the bombs. The intention was to draw the enemy fighters onto us while the main force of our Bombers went to Stettin about 300 miles away. For once, the "Met man" gave us a duff weather forecast. We were supposed to have a strong tail wind helping us to reach the target on time. In fact we met a strong head wind and it needed all the skill of the Pilot and Navigator plus, of course, the efficiency of the Lancaster Bomber to make the ETA. Five of our force had to turn back as they couldn't make it on time. Only seven of us made it. Knowing we were supposed to be sitting ducks made me, if that were possible, even more vigilant. I scoured the sky from port to starboard looking for any sign of the enemy. It was strange over the target. Was our Skipper deliberately inviting enemy action? He pretended to be flying about six bombers calling out false instructions to fool the enemy. I often wonder if he did. Lady Luck, or was it Divine intervention? We saw no enemy fighters, no searchlights and I shall never know why, but not even flak! Perhaps Sylvia's guardian angels were watching over me on her birthday! (Prior to the reprint of this book I discovered why the enemy had been so unusually silent that night. A Polish student contacted me via the RAF Association and informed me that his parents, who lived near the airfield at Schneidemuhl, told him that the Germans had abandoned the airfield prior to the raid! I thanked him for his interest and sent him a signed copy of this book.)

The weather was pretty awful over the next few days and operations were suspended. Christmas Eve arrived and we had a party in the Sergeant's Mess. All Officers were invited too and what a party it was! Towards the end of the evening when most were rather 'tiddly' we finished up singing bawdy songs and cutting each other's ties below the knot. Weren't we daft as well as barmy? Afterwards Harry and I made our way back to our beds. We awoke the next morning not feeling like going on Parade. I can't remember who suggested it but we both agreed that our Flight Commander would be suffering from a hangover and therefore unable to take the Parade. Not a bit of it. Our Navigator Len came into our billet, sent by the Commander to get us up. Everyone looked terrible and the Parade was eventually dismissed

January 1st, 1945 – the weather broke at last and we reported for Operations. The target this time the Mittelland Canal at Gravenhorst in Germany. One hundred bombers took part and we were in the air for 7 hours and 20 minutes. Take off time 1645 hours. Bomb load was 12,000 lbs and we flew in at 11,400 ft. An uneventful trip going, we saw one searchlight, no enemy fighters and only sporadic flak. Coming back was another story however. The weather deteriorated and it started to snow rather heavily, so bad in fact that our base was closed and we were diverted to a place called Milltown. In my heart I was more scared of the elements than of the enemy. True, I had not seen much enemy action but I was always afraid bad weather would make us crash. I knew of one occasion when all airfields were snowbound and the planes that were flying had to head out over the North Sea and the crews bale out which of course meant ditching the aircraft into the sea.

January 5th – the penultimate Operation for us. The allied advance was now making headway. Most of France had been liberated leaving a pocket of the enemy cut off on the Atlantic Coast, part of which was Bordeaux. Our target was troop concentrations at Rouen just outside Bordeaux. At the briefing we were told it was to be a night raid, the RAF was to go in first and the American Air Force would follow us in. I believe this was the first night raid by the Americans. We carried 14 x 1000 lb bombs and were to fly in at 12,000 ft. This was supposed to be an easy raid, identification lights on until the target was almost reached. The enemy wasn't supposed to have many anti-aircraft guns, ammunition or fighters. How wrong we were! I now know what is meant by 'all hell let loose'. Relaxing in my turret – what a stupid thing to do – I was simply going through the motions of searching when BANG, our aircraft shook, and I could hear enemy flak opening up on us. Imagination certainly plays tricks on your eyesight for, on looking to starboard, I could have sworn I was seeing a flight of Bombers close to us. The Bombers turned out to be enemy flak and by now I was fully alert and all I could think was "Let's get the hell out of here." Jock our Bomb Aimer started his bomb run calling "Left, left, steady, right a bit." The plane was vibrating and I could still hear the flak exploding. Jock called out "Dummy run." My heart sank as I knew we had to go round again. We realised the enemy had guns on both sides of the river. I felt that Bordeaux must have been a storage dump for all the anti-aircraft guns and ammunition in France. Nevertheless, we did go round again and dropped our bombs on target. We also managed to return to base without any damage or casualties – not so for some of the lads.

Two days later we were to undertake our twelfth and final Operation.

RAF Lancaster being loaded with a "Blockbuster" bomb

7

After the Crash and Beyond

... **January 8th, 1945** – Dawn broke and I was still alone. The help I had been expecting had not arrived. Thinking I was the only survivor I decided I must not stay here as alone and unaided I knew I would die. Somehow I managed to crawl in the right direction as I had found a path. I chose to turn left passing a woodsman's hut when suddenly I heard, not very far away, church bells ringing. Making a supreme effort I started to crawl in the general direction of this sound. Then, feeling I could go no further, I rested by another tree and after a while I called out feebly "Help, help." Thank God, looking up I saw my saviours rushing towards me. Not knowing how they would react I kept repeating "RAF – English."

With great care I was carried to a house in the village where I later learned that a woman had given me a boiled egg to eat and the men who carried me to safety had given me a glass of Mirabelle, a local alcoholic drink. Both fortified me.

Waiting for an ambulance I was made comfortable and I remember telling the woman by sign language to cut off the flying boot from my injured foot. I could tell by her expression she didn't want to destroy the boot, but my foot hurt agonisingly when she tried to remove it.

All the luck was on my side now as I was only three miles from a fully equipped American Hospital at Commercy. Within hours I was lying in a nice warm clean hospital bed. Penicillin was injected into me every four hours as my injured foot had frostbite and gangrene was setting in. At times I thought the injections within minutes of each other, not realising I was sleeping between the injections. An American doctor came to me and explained that part of my right foot might have to be amputated due to gangrene. I had also punctured my right lung and dislocated my right shoulder which was now in a splint. He then gave me some great news. Harry was alive though badly burned.

Harry had had a premonition that we were going to crash, and grabbed an upright strut that connected to the perspex Astrodome, a lookout point. With great determination he climbed through the hole caused by the perspex melting, some onto him. He then dropped onto the remaining part of the wing and then to the ground. After wandering around for hours he eventually came to a farm about half a mile from where I was taken. The farmer thought at first he was a German and held a pitchfork against his chest.

Within days the news about Harry was even better. The same doctor said Harry's facial burns were only superficial and would leave no permanent scars. Burns to his hand and the back of his legs were more serious and he has suffered from these ever since.

Apart from the kindness shown to me by the American doctors and patients, the thing I remembered most was the food – it was out of this world. Bear in mind that in England we were on rations of 2oz butter a week and small amounts of meat and sugar. Fruit was very scarce, and people queued for bread and cigarettes. Here was I being served good portions of all kinds of food on a plastic tray. A Canadian nurse would visit me daily and make me a cup of tea using a tea bag, the first time I had ever seen one.

Gangrene had taken too strong a hold on my leg and surgeons were compelled to amputate half of my foot, leaving my big toe so that hopefully I would be able to walk again. After a few more days of rest and treatment I was sent home to England. An ambulance conveyed me to the railway station and I was carried to a bunk on a hospital train. Incredibly it was just like a hospital – plenty of electric lights and clean sheets with hospital staff and equipment readily available. On the way to Cherbourg the train stopped overnight at Paris. Not being able to get out I promised myself I would revisit Paris one day. The ship I was carried onto was a Liberty boat built in the hundreds by the Americans. My stretcher must have been placed over the engines because the vibration was giving me hell. Nurses sprayed my leg with scent as the gangrene was still with me and giving off an obnoxious odour.

We docked at Southampton, ENGLAND. My England. From here the train took me to an American Hospital near Winchester. What a difference to the French train, I could have been in a cattle truck for all I knew, cold and damp. Never mind, I soon found myself in similar surroundings to the hospital in Commercy. Again the Americans were fantastic to me, plenty of good food and attention. If only our boys could have known how the "Yanks" looked after me. It's no secret that our boys disliked the 'Yanks'. They had plenty of money, cigarettes, whisky and food, while our lads were poor in comparison. We disliked them for the wrong reasons. It wasn't their fault that we as a nation couldn't afford to 'keep up with the Jones' or, in this case, the 'Yanks'.

Over the years I have regretted not being able to get in touch with these kind Americans. Unfortunately two German POWs carrying me up the gang plank had slipped and my personal belongings, including addresses, fell into the sea.

It was now mid-February and looking outside from my hospital bed I noticed the sun was shining and the snow had gone. Winter was nearly over and already I was beginning to feel better. A doctor came to me and said I was being transferred to an RAF hospital at Wroughton in Swindon, Wiltshire. The driver, a RAF Corporal, helped carry me on a stretcher to his ambulance and I began to realise that soon I would be able to contact my family.

The sun was shining with a nip in the air. I was well wrapped up with blankets all around me. After about two hours the driver asked if I was hungry. I knew I was feeling better because I did. He stopped some way out in the countryside at a large inn.

Within minutes he came back with the owner who smiled and asked how I was. The meal was great – well cooked and with apple pie and custard for pudding, my favourite. After a brief rest the driver set off and we soon arrived at St. Margaret's RAF Hospital in Swindon, Wiltshire. How I loved that place! The doctors, sisters and nurses were so kind. They made everyone feel really comfortable and showed great care. Within a couple of days Doctor Evans came to see me. He arranged for screens to be put around my bed and, sitting beside me, explained about my injured foot and the gangrene. Very kindly he broke the news that even if they could save my foot I would always have trouble with it. He recommended I have it amputated just above the ankle.

It was only then that it hit me, all I could think of was that I would never be able to play football or dance again. I really felt sorry for myself. Yes – I cried unashamedly. A young nurse who had been told my bad news came over to me "Please have something to eat" she said. "I have brought you a boiled egg with bread and butter."

"I couldn't eat it," I said, "even if the King of England asked me." Minutes later I had eaten it! I often smile about this side of my character.

If cowardice spreads panic then bravery or guts, as I have previously said, rub off. Two examples spring to mind. A Navigator who crashed in Burma had both his arms and legs amputated at the scene of the crash to save his life. Surely this man had faith in God and a grateful heart – he never grumbled and was so glad to be alive. I doubt that I could have coped as well as he did.

The other case concerns a man whose face will remain in my memory forever. His name was Smith and he came from Manchester but we called him Smudge. He was helping another man to carry a small German bomb when it went off. His colleague lost both his legs below the knee, but Smudge being a little chap had shrapnel wounds covering his legs from foot to thigh. The doctors said he would never walk again. How he proved them wrong. I had the privilege of talking to him and watched as he progressed from being a bed patient to using a wheelchair, then crutches and finally a walking stick. What courage, what grit! I was, and remain, proud to have known him. Ever since knowing Smudge I have become intolerant of moaners.

The third day proved to be a tonic. It was about 11 o'clock in the morning when I heard footsteps and, looking up, to my utter joy I saw my mother and father. They had received a telegram the day after I crashed saying I was missing, presumed killed. It is only when you are a parent that you can appreciate the anguish one goes through with this kind of message. Fortunately, within a day a further telegram arrived telling them I was in an American hospital somewhere in France. My father who worked at the Post Office in Birmingham had told his superiors, and a colleague called Miss Alcock made numerous phone calls for my parents and as soon as they ascertained I was in Swindon they made their way down immediately. Trying to be brave I said something that hurt my father. My good leg was under the sheets but my injured leg was lying on top. The leg was plastered showing my big toe. "Dad," I said, "that toe is the only one I've got."

My eldest sister came to see me the next day with Sylvia my girlfriend. Elsie told me my father was very upset because he believed I had lost one leg and half of my other foot. I quickly wrote a letter saying how stupid I'd been. It should have taught me to be careful not to say things which could be misconstrued but it is so easily done and a lot of people often make this sad human error.

It is hard to believe but, at times, I was glad to go to the operating theatre. I knew that after an injection I would go to sleep. One day I awoke after my foot was amputated thinking, "Oh, they haven't taken it off." I could still feel my injured foot and the carbuncle I'd had since I was about 15. I soon knew the amputation had been carried out, however. Even now more

43

than forty years afterwards I can still feel my foot and carbuncle at times. Phantom pains they call them. A week later, and just before my 20th birthday, I was allowed home on crutches.

I well remember visiting my Aunt Floss and Uncle Bill who lived in Yardley, a nice suburb then on the outskirts of Birmingham. When I was a young boy I used to go to parties at their house. I was then one of ten children, all under fourteen years old, with me being the fourth eldest. They were very kind to us kids. I was walking on crutches towards their house when another man passed me on crutches. I looked at him closely and noticed one of his legs had been amputated at his thigh. He could not wear an artificial leg and he was about 45 years old. What struck me most was how quickly he walked and with so little effort. Here was I labouring and walking with difficulty. I could not understand at the time that I was still not 100% fit. Also I must confess that I have always been a little impatient, to say the least.

A new hospital had been opened in Birmingham, the Queen Elizabeth. Today it reminds me of a village, very big with many buildings. The authorities said I could be transferred to this hospital if I wished. I thought about it a lot and decided I wished to stay at Swindon. I was so happy with the attention and treatment I was receiving plus the fact I needed, and would possibly miss, the companionship of Smudge and the other patients with whom I experienced empathy.

About three weeks after the amputation, on my return to Swindon, my stump had still not healed so Dr Evans said it would be best if I had a re-amputation still leaving about seven inches below the knee. By now I had complete faith in him and said, "You're the doctor."

Sylvia and I had decided by now that we wanted to get engaged. The Sister in charge of the ward was wonderful to me. She organised a little party with a smashing cake. She also taught me that there is a beauty beyond the senses – she was no Aphrodite but she had a beautiful spirit and was the most caring person I have ever known.

44

The day arrived for me to be discharged from hospital. My stump had healed and I had full use of my knee. I had come to terms with the fact that I would need to wear an artificial leg. Thinking the leg would be made quickly Sylvia and I decided to get married on November 24th. A community hall was booked for the reception, bridesmaids selected, as well as the church. Unfortunately the new leg was not ready and I had to get married on crutches. I had decided to wear my RAF uniform and I was very pleased when the photographer was able to take the photos making it appear I had two legs!

Ron and Sylvia – 24th November 1945

During the reception I was a little disappointed seeing couples dancing while I had to sit and watch. Nevertheless it made me more determined than ever to overcome my difficulty. If Smudge could walk so could I.

The Wedding Group

Sylvia and I were very fortunate in that we managed to rent a self-contained flat at 512A Holly Lane, Erdington. The RAF Association gave me an interest-free loan to help with the furniture.

At last in February 1946 I was able to collect my first artificial leg. I felt like a kid at Christmas with a new toy. Walking to a tram stop I noticed people weren't staring at me like they used to when I was using crutches. I remember going along to an Association where I went on to become the Secretary, The Birmingham and Midland Limbless Ex-Servicemen's Association – later known as BLESMA. I went initially to be shown how to walk. A committee member introduced himself saying he would teach me to walk properly. After walking up and down the room twice he said "Young man you can walk better than I can."

Over the years I have taken great delight knowing people have not realised I wear an artificial leg as, in my younger days, I was able to play cricket, football and golf, dance and climb ladders – I am still able to drive a car. A young boy in his early teens who lived near Sylvia's parents lost his leg in a car accident. He knew I wore a false leg and though we never spoke his eyes never left me when I was near him. Somehow I knew he was saying to himself, "One day I shall walk like him." I watched him later climb trees and lamp posts. I like to think that I helped him to overcome his disability.

Harry and I hadn't met since the crash and I was so excited when, at last, he arranged to visit us. We met at Snow Hill station which doesn't exist now. I thought he had missed the train as I could not see him after all the passengers had gone. He hadn't noticed me waiting and had walked past me. It was only when he retraced his steps that we met. It was such an emotional meeting. I could hardly believe it was him. A few months earlier he was a young man with black hair, now he was white-haired. I suppose this was one of the rotten things about war – it made young people old before their time. How I envy the teenagers of today. After this we always kept in close touch with one another. He married Winnie and after a while they adopted David and emigrated to New Zealand. Unfortunately Winnie died and Harry decided to come back to England. I arranged to meet Harry and David at Southampton and brought them to my home. After spending a couple of days with us, I drove them to visit Winnie's sister who lived in Barrow-in-Furness. Soon afterwards Harry met and married Betty and they settled down in Sheffield.

8

Life after the RAF

After my discharge from the RAF I now had to think about going back to work. To tell the truth I was scared – I had lost my confidence. I didn't know what type of work would suit me. I went along to the Labour Office and immediately fell foul of the Clerk who dealt with me. He offered me a menial low-paid job and when I asked if he had a better paid job for me he retorted "Well, you've got your War Pension to supplement your wages haven't you?" I responded angrily saying that my pension was compensation for my wartime sacrifices not a supplement to a miserly wage offer!

At first my pension was ten shillings and eight pence (53p today!). I accepted this was fair as the country was in debt just after the War. Not getting satisfaction at the Labour Office I went to find a job on my own initiative. There were plenty of jobs, in fact one could leave one job in the morning and start another in the afternoon. In this respect we were lucky. After working as an assembler at a couple of firms in the city, I went along to Ansells Brewery at Aston Cross. They were looking for someone to work in their Accounts Office. I am not being conceited when I say I was very good at mental arithmetic, my favourite subject. I was given a written test and was told that the job was mine at £5 per week. For a few seconds I was elated but then disappointed when he checked and informed me that £5 was only for someone aged 25. By this time Sylvia was pregnant with Susan and I knew I couldn't afford to accept the rate of £3.50 so I declined their offer. The same afternoon I went to Moss Gear on the Chester Road at Erdington not far from my home. At first I started as an assembler making special gear boxes for lorries but I found it too strenuous and luckily was transferred to the Production Office as a Progress Clerk. At last I had a job I liked and all through my life I have said to numerous people how important it is to have a job that one enjoys.

On December 3rd 1946, Sylvia gave birth to our first child Susan, or Sue as we have always called her. It was a difficult labour and the midwife called in our GP Dr. Sudki to assist her. He was of Egyptian origin and had two practices. He must have been over 70 then and practiced into his 90s! I had great faith in him and it was through his efforts that Sue was eventually born after a 36 hour labour without any serious problems. I was highly delighted but the waiting did affect my nerves, so much so that five years later when Sylvia was carrying Renny our son, the midwife Sister Ashton arranged for Sylvia to go to the Women's Hospital in Moseley. The reason she gave was that it was for my benefit due to my nervousness when Sue was born!

In January, 1947, we had a very severe winter. Transport stopped and fuel couldn't reach the factories or homes. Food was short, businesses closed down and ours was one of them. Everyone was laid off. It was a very bad spell. My mother-in-law was great visiting us every Thursday during this period and bringing with her a shopping bag full of coal. You have to understand that this journey involved catching a tram from Northfield to Birmingham Navigation Street, a good three quarters of a mile walk across the city to Steelhouse Lane, another tram to Holly Lane, and a ten minute walk to our flat. She was as good as gold!

One Thursday Sylvia's mother told us that she had seen a bedroom suite at a furniture store in the city centre at a sale price of £40. The sale was to commence at 0900 hrs on Saturday. I was very keen to purchase this suite so the following day, Friday, I went to work prepared to camp outside the store all night. Armed with a sleeping bag and a flask of coffee I arrived at the store about 1700 hrs. I made my way inside and asked to see the manager. On telling him that I wished to purchase that particular suite he said that if I was the first customer on

Saturday morning the suite would indeed be mine. When I responded that I was staying overnight until the store opened he immediately invited me into his Warehouse and said I could have any of the other sale suites on show. Thanking him I said my heart was set on that particular suite.

After everyone had gone home and the store closed I made myself comfortable for the night. Luckily there was a covered entrance to the store so I was not affected by the elements. During the night a policeman came along, shone his torch on me and demanded to know what I was doing there. He not only accepted my explanation but said he would pass a message on to his colleagues so that I would not be disturbed. He was true to his word. When the store opened at 0900 hrs there was another couple there who had arrived about 0840 hrs. On being told that I had been there all night they went away muttering that it was a fiddle. Whenever we wanted anything for the house, carpets, furniture, etc., I would always wait for a store to have a sale. During my life I have found that, no matter how well off people are, we all like a bargain.

After about 15 months I saw an internal job advertised for a Buyer and applied for it. To discourage me from taking the job my boss said that the salary was less than what I was already getting. Now full of confidence in my ability I said that I didn't care for the limited prospects on offer in my current post and I gave him a week's notice. This was another turning point in my life and one that I have never regretted.

There was a shadow factory in Castle Bromwich that comprised eight separate buildings – very big indeed. After the War it closed down. As I remember Fort Dunlop rented one building and the G.P.O. part of another. A firm called Fisher and Ludlow had a number of little factories near to the city centre. They specialised in making car body pressings, beer crates, sinks and wash basins. Having a lot of foresight the Chairman, a Mr. Arthur Keats, decided to move to Castle Bromwich. Mr. Keats was one of the few men who earned my respect. He was a good man. My luck was truly in when I called at Fisher & Ludlow's Labour Office. I was interviewed by a Mr. Harry Thorpe, another nice man. Whether it was pity or not I do not know but he gave me a job as a Progress Clerk in a department making washing machines. Mr. Keats and other outside businessmen decided to make the Bendix Washing Machine under license from Bendix America. The wages were over £8 per week. Was I glad I had called in there! The icing on the cake, however, was the twice yearly bonus that was paid to salaried and non-production workers in July and December. It was quite substantial, so much so that we were able to go on holiday in the summer and also buy presents and have a good Christmas. The good days had started! Those were the happiest days of my working life. Each day I reported the shortages or problems to either Production Control who made many items in-house, or to the Buying Office who purchased components from outside. I also reported daily to the General Manager and to the Works Manager. What a job!

One Saturday morning when I got out of bed to go to work I had a problem, my stump that fits into a socket on my artificial leg, now called a prosthesis, was so swollen I couldn't put the leg on. I immediately went to the Limb Fitting Centre and arrangements were made for me to go to a military hospital in Worcester. A week later I was home but unable to wear the prosthesis for four more weeks. Mr. Arthur Harper the General Manager sent a car for me and asked if I would go to work on crutches. I was so happy at work that I agreed. Some of my workmates were shocked to see me on crutches with a leg missing. They thought I had been in a car accident! Not many people knew that I wore a prosthesis as I truly did walk well. Having my own knee did help of course. I was as happy as a sandboy. One of our customers was a firm in New Zealand called Fisher Paykel. Food, fruit and chocolates were still in short supply and one day food parcels arrived from New Zealand. I was fortunate to receive one. Sylvia and I made the most of this unexpected luxury.

One day Mr. Harper sent for me and asked me to transfer to the Buying Office. Production was going up and they needed another Buyer. It is true I was made welcome by the Section Leader, but I wasn't happy. I hated being cooped up all day in a large office. This was a staff job. How delighted I was when Mr. Harper sent for me again and asked me to take over the Bendix Production Stores. I'd never worked in Stores but over the months I learned the basic principles of Stock Control. When someone in the Buying Office said he didn't think this was promotion, one of my colleagues asked "Is it more money?" to which I answered "Yes." "Then it is a promotion," was the reply.

As production grew to approximately 500 machines per week so did the demand for spares. In fact after about 12 months I was asked to organise and run a Spare Parts Stores. I truly enjoyed setting up new Stores and putting in my systems. A certain Ken Loft was transferred to me as a junior foreman. Ken was, and is, a great fellow. We still keep in touch even though we are now 80 years old – a true friend indeed. (Shortly before the reprint of this book we both attended each other's 90th birthday celebrations!)

Life is full of ups and downs and when you are down there is only one way to go and that is up. I say this because I never trusted my new boss. In my opinion he was a proper Jekyll and Hyde, nice to your face when someone else was there but really nasty at other times.

As the business grew in strength a firm of consultants was called in. Apart from paperwork systems salary scales were introduced, rates of pay for Production Inspection, Maintenance and Progress and Stores. Unfortunately Stores was the lowest scale but on reflection this was correct. However, I did become upset when I found out that the two junior foremen who worked for me were on the same salary as me. Believing that this was not fair I asked for an interview with my boss. I'm afraid it didn't end very well. He flatly refused to discuss my salary saying he would only give me a rise when he decided to increase everyone else's. I informed him that I wasn't happy with his explanation and I asked to see the Personnel Manager, Mr. Barry Mackie. This time he could not refuse my request. Mr. Mackie listened to my complaint and said "We don't work like that here" referring to the comment "You will get a rise when everyone else does." Another fair man. Of course my boss wasn't very happy about the result and our relationship, to say the least, became very strained. In the main, however, he left me alone.

It was about this time that our son Renny was born, September 24th 1952 to be exact, at the Sorrento Nursing Home in Acocks Green. Sylvia has always been an avid reader and at the time was reading a series of books by Mazo de la Roche called the "Whiteoaks Story." Renny was one of the characters and Sylvia fell in love with the name.

At home life had become a problem. As I have said previously, the flat only had one main bedroom and a small second bedroom with just enough room for a single bed and was no longer suitable for a family of four. After much deliberation Sylvia and I decided that we must try and buy a house. Birmingham like other big cities had a major housing shortage. As we were in a flat, even though it was now no longer suitable, we knew that we had no chance of getting a house from the Corporation Housing Estate. There were thousands much worse off than us.

We heard that a new development was taking place in a village called Northfield, the land owned by Bourneville Village Trust. During this period builders had to have a permit and even then they could only build twelve houses. This restriction was lifted before our house was built. One of the builders lived near us in Erdington so Sylvia and I went along and were allowed to pick our own plot. My eldest brother Ted and his wife Jean also became interested and asked us to pick a plot for them. When we came away from the builders we were extremely elated. Our dream of owning a house now became a distinct possibility. Time was on our side because we were told that it

53

would take at least six months to complete. We saw a solicitor who arranged our mortgage, supposedly 100% over 25 years. The price of the house was £1,770 – a lot of money then!

One day Sylvia telephoned me at work. She was with her mother in "Rackhams" and had fallen in love with some green velvet curtains that she thought would look lovely in our new lounge. I readily agreed that she could buy them.

As the time drew near to sign the contract, a bombshell was dropped. The solicitor got in touch to say that the Building Society would now only give us 95% – we would have to pay £89. I told him that I had not budgeted for that and had spent all of our savings on furniture, carpets and curtains. The solicitor came up trumps and, after a 'phone call, informed us that the Co-op Building Society would provide 100% mortgage with 5% of this covered by an endowment policy. I could have kissed him! Ted came with me to finalise his purchase of a similar house around the corner four doors away. I guess we were both lucky that we didn't have adjoining plots as I truly believe both families needed a bit of space from each other. We were both satisfied.

Imagine how we all felt when the plan showed a three bedroom house with a large kitchen, lounge dining room and bathroom, as well as space at the side for a garage to be built. Of course we knew that it would be a long time before we could even think of buying a car. Every week on a Sunday Sylvia, Susan, Renny and I would catch the trams from Erdington to see how the house was progressing. Sometimes we were in the doldrums when little action seemed to have taken place, at other times we were so happy to see the house taking shape.

As I was on staff I was able to pick one week's holiday of my choice and, of course, I saved it for the week of the move. The work did drag on and I had to keep postponing my week's holiday. For some reason the final touches kept being put off, so much so that I said to Sylvia, "I am going to move into the new house in two weeks' time even if it isn't finished!" The house wasn't finished but the painter who worked for the builder was very sympathetic and gave us a key to the house. It is difficult to imagine how happy we were. When we moved in there was this brand new house decorated and carpeted throughout, and with velvet full length curtains across the entire 15'4" width of the lounge. I felt at times that I was dreaming.

* * * * *

More Changes at Work

Production was still around 500 washing machines per week. This meant that the Spares Department was now a big concern so the Directors decided to take it away from the Production side and transfer its functions to the Bendix Service Manager. His job was to provide Service Engineers to install, maintain and fit spares as and when needed. The Planning Department became involved and I was asked to liaise with them. A separate single-storey building near to the factory was selected for the new Spares Department although half of the building was occupied by the Fisher and Ludlow Apprentice Department. A two-storey row of bins was erected with a conveyor running all round the binned area. An air operated hoist was erected at two extreme corners and the conveyor carried a trolley that held a storage tin. When an order was completed the relevant tin of spares would drop onto a metal roller track. Work benches were placed along this track where checkers and panel packers worked. I was very pleased when the Service Manager asked me to transfer to him.

Some months after we moved saw the end of the Bendix Production Line at Castle Bromwich. Unemployment was very high in Liverpool and with Government intervention production was transferred to Liverpool with selected members of the staff being transferred. Unfortunately the move was not a success as labour problems were taking place with absenteeism and falling sales. The Director decided to shut this factory down and production ceased. Later Bendix washing machines and fridges were made under licence by manufacturers in Italy.

The wheel had turned full circle and instead of a sellers' market it was now a buyers' market. Many firms were now making domestic goods and cars with more goods being made by a lot more manufacturers than were being sold. Allied to this was the Union power that unfortunately posed serious threats to the stability of many companies.

After about five years, when production of the washing machine had ceased, it was decided to move the Spares Department to a site at Saltley away from the main factory. I had decided in my own mind that if I wasn't offered the job of Superintendent I did not wish to work for someone else. Remember that I had grown up with the Spares Department and truly believed that I had earned the right to be promoted. I was therefore naturally disappointed when one of the Service Engineers was given the job. I wrote a letter to my boss, the Service Manager, saying that I didn't wish to be transferred from Fisher and Ludlow to Bendix Home Appliances. I did promise him that I would ensure that the transfer of the Spares Department would be a success. I kept my word and the transfer was smoothly carried out. When I approached my boss he was most surprised to hear me say that I was serious when I said I had no wish to be transferred. He thought I was trying it on to get more money.

This was another chapter ending with the loss of work for me, but I was no longer afraid of the future.

Our first view of Méligny-le-Grand

View of Méligny-le-Grand from the forest crash site

Ron, Andre, Harry, Tom
and the Memorial Plaque

Harry and Ron at the
Memorial Stone

The Memorial Stone
at the crash site

Ron and Harry with Harry's painting
"Bonjour Méligny" outside St. Evre

Ron beside rear turret of saved Lancaster bomber

Ron in Francis' museum holding one of his four machine guns

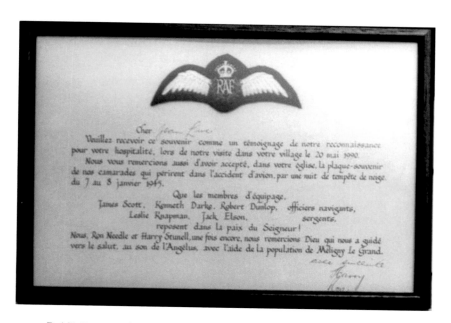

RAF Remembrance Plaque presented by Ron and Harry

André with his extended family

André's daughter Catherine
(the photographer)

The cakes!

9

Another New Beginning

Naturally life had its problems at our new home. It was now taking me over two and a half hours travelling to and from work. This did not bother me as it was our choice to move back to Northfield and it was the right decision. Mind you, I was a selfish person. Here was me thinking that because I was the breadwinner Sylvia should not complain. It wasn't a bed of roses for her. She would get up very early after I had taken her a cup of tea in bed, something I have always done. What I didn't think about was the dressing and feeding of Renny who was under two years old, taking Susan to school morning and afternoon whilst pushing Renny in a pushchair. Every night when I arrived home from work, no matter what the time, my dinner would be placed before me, piping hot with a nice cup of tea. It was years before I realised that she had made more sacrifices than me. I tried to make up for it later in life.

Sylvia and I spoke and smiled many times at an incident that took place one night in the winter when I was returning home. It was very cold with ice and snow on the ground. When I got off the tram at Whitehill Lane, near to the Royal Orthopaedic Hospital, an elderly man spoke to me. He said "Excuse me, do you think you could help me to walk down the lane?" – the lane was very steep and treacherous. He was using a stick and was very apprehensive. I replied, "Of course I will," and I allowed him to hold my arm until he arrived at his door. Little did he realise that the man helping him only had one leg!

When Sue and Renny reached the ages of eleven and five respectively Sylvia returned to paid employment. A new school had opened nearby for children with learning difficulties, many of whom had cerebral palsy or problems with mobility. Sylvia helped to feed one young boy who was unable to feed himself.

She enjoyed this because the young boy would get excited when he saw Sylvia and give her a lovely smile. One day the boy's grandmother came to our house and thanked Sylvia for being so kind. This made us both contented.

My brother-in-law and dear friend Reg had taught me to drive in an old Austin Ruby 7. Sometimes my younger brother Brian had also helped me. One summer Reg, his wife Ruby and their two children "little" Reg and Ro, Sylvia and I with Sue and Renny, went to Torquay in Devon for a holiday. Somehow we all got into his car. I tell this little story because I remember Reg saying to the car when we were going up a hill "Mush, Mush" as if he was driving a sledge led by huskie dogs! Since we first met Ruby and Reg have always been very close to Sylvia and me. We were special friends.

When I was around 30 we were in a position to buy a car, or should I say a "van"? Austin Motors of Longbridge, quite near to us, were making a van called the "A35." It had rear passenger seats but no rear-side windows. The van was blue and the registration 'XOA 356' – the price was £365. I believe most drivers remember the registration of their first vehicle. There was a scheme at work that allowed employees to purchase Austin and Morris motorcars with a good discount. In those days a vehicle could be sold after 12 months at approximately the same price one had paid for it. That was what I did.

This was another chapter in our lives. We were now able to socialise more and sometimes, together with my siblings and their families who lived nearby, we would go out on trips at the weekends to places like Symonds Yat in Herefordshire, Warwick Park, Evesham and many more. There would be about five cars in convoy! I used to smile because Ted my eldest brother would follow the leader but when we were near to our destination he would overtake everyone in order to be the first to arrive – even on the return journey! Most weekends we would also visit Sylvia's mum and dad and stay for tea. Sylvia's dad and I got on very well. He could play the banjo and we would enjoy many 'sing-alongs'. He was very intelligent and would often amaze me with his knowledge. One day one of Sylvia's friends who liked opera visited her parents' home. Pop, as I called him, was able to hold a conversation with her about this subject. As someone said, "Life is an education" and it surely is.

My second vehicle was a new white mini – BOP151. It truly was a car of the period. Sylvia and I, Renny, Susan and her friend went on holiday to Hemsby near Gt. Yarmouth. I still cannot believe that this mini was able to take all five of us plus all our luggage. No roof rack! Those were the years that I loved to drive. How sad that as we grow older it ceases to be a pleasure. In my case I think it's because I have to concentrate more which makes me become tired very quickly.

At our local park a Pitch and Putt golf course was made available. In the summer Ted, Ken another brother, Ken Laight (my sister Gladys' husband) and I went there most nights of the week for a game. How I wished later on in life that I had had a few golf lessons. It was my favourite pastime. I realised after a few years that I was making the same mistake time and time again. This was the reason I told myself because I never became a good golfer unlike my younger brother Don who, some years later, played to a low handicap even when he hadn't played for many months! Mind you I realised that for a one legged player I was doing remarkably well. A group of us from work formed a Golfing Section. We called ourselves "The Road Runners." Each Whitsun we would have a three day golfing holiday at Coleford Golf Club in the Wye Valley. Reg and my brother Don also joined. How grateful and proud I was to say that I was able to play 64 holes of golf in those three days. Sometimes my stump was raw and bleeding from the effort but I healed well and recovered quite quickly. However, later in life I once again felt selfish at times thinking of Sylvia back home with the family unable to share the experience. I had so many happy years of playing golf – it was, and is, my favourite sport. I love to watch it on TV.

I must mention the camaraderie between "The Road Runners." In the group were two Irish lads from Belfast, one a Catholic and the other a Protestant. They, like the rest of us, didn't ask each other about what religion they followed, we simply accepted each other for what we were. Jack and Derry were the best of friends and very good golfers. How wonderful it would be if everyone ignored colour, different faiths, or even no faith at all. It is how we treat each other that is important – try and be a friend to others and if it is not reciprocated it's their problem, not yours. My sister Ruby used to say "If you smile at someone you usually get a smile in return." I tried it and nine times out of ten it worked. I also like the saying of Dave Allen the Irish comedian (who incidentally was the cousin of Derry, my golfing friend) "MAY YOUR GOD GO WITH YOU."

Derry Hayden was my favourite. He could drink 15 pints a night and yet wasn't a bit aggressive – in fact he was very funny. But the sad truth is that in his 60s he lost both his legs because of his drinking and died shortly afterwards. One of the reasons I liked him was because he wasn't a scrounger. At our weekend golf breaks we used to have a kitty for the drinks and some would drink more than others. Derry, however, would quickly go to the bar on his own and buy the extra drinks he wanted. All my life I have disliked scroungers, particularly when I know they are not short of a bob or two!

Regrettably old age and shortness of breath forced me to give up golf. I did miss it just as much as I missed dancing the way I could before I lost my leg.

Occasionally I had problems with my artificial leg and found it necessary to visit the Limb Fitting Centre that was now situated in Selly Oak, the next district to where I lived. I would telephone and explain the problem and as I was a war pensioner I would be seen as priority and given an appointment without delay. The staff and fitters were first class and did everything they could to ensure the artificial leg was comfortable. Two events here stand out in my memory.

On the first occasion I was in a room with about six others waiting my turn to see a fitter. In the room were two sets of wooden support rails with a mirror at each end. These enabled someone wearing an artificial leg for the first time to look in the mirror whilst at the same time using the rails for support. This way one could adjust one's steps or see if the leg was fitted properly. On this occasion an elderly man with a full-leg amputation was trying his leg on for the first time. After a few steps he came back and sat on the chair at the end of the walkway. The doctor accompanying him asked what the problem was. The man's exact words were "It's copping me here" pointing to a spot at the top and between his legs. Much to the amusement of everyone there the doctor replied, "You mean – your balls?" "Yes" was the reply.

On the second occasion I had been asked to attend with a request to bring my spare leg with me. Luckily I hadn't had a problem with my leg for years. When the doctor looked at my spare leg he said, "Oh dear, we will have to condemn this leg." Immediately I retorted "You can't do that – it's my favourite leg." He simply smiled and said, "Alright, we'll get the fitter to have a look at it." Aren't there a lot of nice people about?

Sitting next to me on one of my visits was a man a little older than myself but with the same disability. He asked me if I belonged to the Birmingham and Midland Limbless Association. Having informed him that I did once but not now an invitation to rejoin was made to me and I readily accepted. Sylvia and I became so involved that it has, and still does, play an important part in our lives. It's impossible to put into words the comradeship and camaraderie we all experienced except to say that everyone got on so well together – no-one spoke about how they received their injuries.

Our Vice Chairman had a daughter who worked for a National Hotel group. She was able to get us cheap weekend bookings at three to five star hotels. The Association is a charity and the Birmingham Business Fraternity make generous donations that enable us to have almost free holidays at the weekends. I hope that Judy and Martin Dyke will forgive me for mentioning their names but they do such a lot, not only for our Association but other worthwhile causes.

In the early 1990s the National British Limbless Ex Servicemens' Association opened a branch known as the Birmingham and Solihull Branch of B.L.E.S.M.A. Many of us had the best of both worlds belonging to both Associations. BLESMA have two homes, one in Blackpool and the other in Crieff, Scotland. Members as well as their wives, and widows were allowed to spend two weeks twice a year at the home for a nominal fee. Later in life when old age and my war disability deteriorated the War Pensions Department paid not only my fee but also gave me a generous travel allowance. I am not being flippant when I say 'losing one's leg does have its advantages'!

Sylvia and I always enjoyed Crieff where there was only ever a maximum of 10 residents with up to 35 rooms available for visitors. We were always welcomed with open arms. Nothing remains the same though and as we grew older there were fewer of us visiting Crieff. To compensate for this the Home increased the residents to around 20. Nevertheless we have been going twice a year for over 15 years and the staff and carers have always been kind and considerate.

10

Fate

Life at work had now entered its last chapter. Isn't fate strange? All through my life fate in the main has been good to me. Whenever Sylvia and I were short of money, and it happened a few times, something always turned up. So it was with my employment – as the saying goes, "As one door shuts, another one opens." Mind you I do believe that one should go looking for doors that are invitingly open.

The company was now employing about 5,000 people with the emphasis on making car bodies. One block was altered to take bodies in bare metal and after a few processes a complete painted car body was produced. Maintenance and replacements of tracks and equipment was a major concern. There were breakdowns, and nearly all items to maintain the different Blocks came from the Engineering Stores. A great deal of time was being wasted by Maintenance personnel having to go to the Stores. It was taking ten minutes plus for some of the men to get to the Stores, and sometimes they would have to wait in a long queue before being served. The Works Engineer in charge of both Maintenance and Stores knew that I was in between jobs. He asked me if I would take over the Engineering Stores with the emphasis on opening Sub Stores in the different Blocks. It was years after that I realised and accepted that I was a good organiser, but a lousy supervisor! However, it took months before I was satisfied that both Sub and main Stores operated efficiently. Each Sub Store record card was cross referenced with the main Stores locations. When requisitions were sent to the main Stores the Storekeeper knew where to find each item. I knew I was a lousy supervisor because after the system was put in, and Storekeepers knew their jobs, I was bored out of my mind. To tell the truth workers don't need much supervision. If someone doesn't pull their weight their workmates will soon get at them!

Another change was made to the departmental structure when it was decided to merge Progress Despatch and Stores together. Instead of working for the Works Engineer I worked for a Superintendent already established. This was acceptable because the changes made sense to me.

* * * * *

Hindsight

What a wonderful thing to have..... – IF ONLY! Little did our Chairman and others across the country know that, with hindsight, they should have stood up to the militant Unions when excessive demands were made during what I call the "Boom years." I remember well our Chairman saying, "We can afford to give the Unions what they demand." The cost was then added to the sales price which led to the company becoming uncompetitive and eventually closing down. To cite an example:

The Maintenance Department had electricians, machine fitters, pipe fitters, and carpenters. All had mates. When a machine, a lathe, press, milling machine, etc. was fitted or removed, excessive labour was used and unnecessary overtime given. Unions demanded that, when the working week was reduced from 48 to 44 hours, then to 40 and again to 38, maintenance and auxiliary workers needed to still work these extra hours. Even some production workers came in on a Saturday, not to work but to justify their bonus earned during normal hours. Hindsight would have made both Management and Unions act differently. How I envied firms with a Management and Union Committee. They both had the same interests at heart. For our company and some others it was just a battle. I am sure that if Management had informed Unions of the true extent of the problems the situation would have been better.

In the late 1970s firms were cutting back on production and rumours were rife that we were closing down. Another company in our group, based in Swindon, was duplicating what we were making.

At the age of 56 I had now reached a point in my life where I was no longer happy at work. At home the mortgage was paid up, the car was paid for and the children had grown up. After a chat with Sylvia I decided to volunteer for redundancy. I did have another job to go to, nowhere near the same salary, but in my mind it still meant that Sylvia and I could live reasonably well. As I have said before, having a job that you like is so important. If you don't like the job and it is possible, look for another.

While working my month's notice it was officially announced that the firm was going to close. Obviously Swindon was more efficient and cheaper than we were at Castle Bromwich. I was sad because I had worked there for 34 years. It was a great place to work, but like I say, nothing lasts for ever!

I had decided that in future, and for the last few years of my working life, I would only stay at a job that I liked. The money was not the main issue. There is a time in life, around 50 years of age, when I think that people should take stock of themselves and decide what they really want. Money and high wages do not always bring contentment.

My first job was as a rep for an industrial clothing supplier but it didn't work out. Travelling all over England and staying at different hotels didn't suit me, perhaps I was too old. Eventually I went to T.I. Industries as a Production and Stock Controller. A nice title but not much of a salary. Never mind, it was a means to an end. Fifteen months later the Chairman agreed to let me leave when I was 60. I was replaced by one of the existing staff and therefore paid an allowance because someone else had taken my job.

11

Changes As We Grow Older

When we were newlyweds, and for years after, our social life included going to weddings and christenings. As both Sylvia and I came from large families, a lot of our time was spent attending these functions. They were indeed happy days. One of the problems, and it is a big and serious one, is that when you are growing older, instead of christenings and weddings, funerals and hospitals take over. Pop, after he retired, developed cancer and died quite quickly. My mother spent the last few days of her life in Selly Oak Hospital. She had three coronary attacks and knew she was going to die. The way she died helped me to accept losing parents, family and friends, more easily. The night before she died most of my brothers and sisters were at her bedside. My mother was quite cheerful and told us of her wishes for her funeral. Mum passed away that same night.

Just over a year later my father was in the same hospital. The gassing he was subjected to in the First World War had caught up with him. He couldn't breathe without the aid of an oxygen mask. I visited him every day for two to three weeks and one morning I called to see him on my way to work. My dad had a habit of putting his thumb up to show that he was ok, something I caught off him because I do it often. This time he put his thumb up but when I got to work about half an hour later I received a 'phone call to say he had passed away peacefully. Mum and Dad were buried together in the same family grave.

Life wasn't all doom and gloom though. My brothers, sisters and I became very close and socialised together throughout our lives. In fact, apart from my sister Ruby who I saw every week, the rest of our family lived within a mile of each other.

When Sylvia and I were 39 years old she became pregnant with our third child. This, I thought at the time, was rather unfortunate as Susan was 18, Renny 13 and we were beginning to socialise more. I was truly glum but I didn't realise that fate was once again being kind to me.

Maria was born on February 15th, 1964, on a Saturday. Sylvia's mother was there and made a fuss of the baby, as indeed we all did. Ken my brother-in-law and good friend also visited. As well as Maria being born, the day was also memorable due to a water leak in our bedroom. We had had central heating installed and new radiators fitted. The timber floor boards had also been renewed but not put back to our satisfaction. I therefore re-nailed the boards but one nail must have penetrated a pipe. Water suddenly started to drip from the lounge ceiling. As a temporary measure I placed a bucket under the drip. Fortunately we had a good next door neighbour called Lionel who came round and soldered the affected pipe. Luckily no serious damage was done.

12

Retirement

For me retirement was something I had been looking forward to for many years. Sure I know that some people love work. If they are fit enough, want to work and have a job, good luck to them. We are all different though. Fortunately Sylvia and I have not got expensive tastes. We both enjoy our meals and we did and do live well. I couldn't afford to squander money but, at the same time, I didn't have to count the pennies.

At first I was kept busy in the house and garden but age complaints were beginning to catch up with me. Walking up inclines was becoming a problem as I was soon out of breath and golfing was no longer an option. No matter, I had other interests, so I accepted the difficulties and made the most of the life I had. I can't stand moaners.

Between the ages of 60 and 70 I developed coronary heart disease, chronic obstructive airways disease, and bowel trouble with diverticulosis. But I was not in pain. As I said to my doctor after he prescribed seven different types of medication "Thanks Doc for keeping me alive." As my dad said, "Life is sweet." Yes we have our ups and downs in life, but I reckon I have had more ups than downs.

Ruby, Reg, Gladys, Sylvia and I went to our caravan at Symonds Yat most weekends. For a few years it was great fun. Reg liked to cook – give him a glass of wine and he was as happy as a sand boy. We all got on so well. After a while Sylvia and I became more involved with BLESMA and only went to the caravan on the odd occasion. The cost of rent, upkeep and petrol meant that it was now very expensive so we gave up the caravan and did not regret it at all.

More of our leisure time was being taken up with BLESMA including two trips to Crieff in Scotland for a fortnight in both

May and October. If the weather was good that was a bonus! Along with Ruby and Reg and our other friends we always enjoyed ourselves. Our wives had a break as well as us men folk. We were all waited on by a caring staff. The ladies went shopping, the many charity shops were a favourite. Don't we all like a bargain? When we didn't go on coach trips a few of the men went to the local pub called the "Pretoria." The locals made us so welcome. Yes, we did spend a few pounds between us but the generosity was returned. Every holiday the owners of the pub gave us a bottle of good single malt whisky the day before we left. We gave the bottle to the nurse-in-charge at the BLESMA Home to distribute to the elderly war veteran residents who were allowed a tot now and then.

Perhaps I shouldn't say this but I was amused when one of the residents mistakenly thought someone had taken his Zimmer frame. When the actual owner refused to give it to him he was greeted with the remark "I'm going to tell my mum." Old age does play tricks with one's memory! My friendship and love for Scotland made me say, and it is true "If I hadn't been born an Englishman I would have liked to have been born a Scotsman!" People who haven't been to Scotland don't know what they are missing. The scenery needs to be seen to be believed.

Another week in the year our Association would arrange a week's holiday by the sea. Over the years we had used one or two different coach companies but for years we had the pleasure, and I do mean pleasure, of going with a coach company called "Mystic Isles of Droitwich." The company is run and owned by Kevin and Jenny Legg. They are truly caring people who deserve to be blessed in life. On one occasion one of our widows went to the wrong coach station in Digbeth and we set off without her. She somehow managed to phone their offices. Can you believe Kevin arranged for a car to fetch her and to meet up with us at Newbury? On another occasion they wouldn't leave until a taxi arrived to take one of the widows home. They often went out of their way to help their passengers. This reminds me of the compensations in life that follow misfortune – what a lot of nice people I would never have known!

It would be remiss of me not to mention our War Pensions Welfare Officer, Mrs. Linda Stokes who, together with her staff, is at the beck and call of all the War pensioners and widows. If there is one person I know who works beyond the call of duty it is Linda – trips to Weston-Super-Mare, Christmas parties, outings for all of us at some stage in the year. I know that a lot of people are quite rightly honoured for their services. I pray that one day Mrs. Stokes will be rewarded for her efforts.

Regrettably my eldest sister Elsie passed away at Selly Oak Hospital following complications with peritonitis. I was somewhat consoled knowing that she didn't suffer for too long.

My thoughts automatically turn to Ken Laight, my brother-in-law and friend, who died whilst working with me at a factory in the city centre. I had the unpleasant task of telling Gladys, my sister.

Humour has always played an important part in my life. My family and I have always managed to laugh at our own and each other's little misfortunes. One day Sylvia and I were making one of our regular visits to London. We were staying at our daughter Sue's home in Camden Town. Our two granddaughters, Samantha and Sally, together with Maria were with us when we visited Renny.

After exiting Camden Town underground station we saw a bus and ran to catch it. Sylvia and the others were waiting for me at the bus stop. However, they had to wait a little longer! The strap holding my prosthetic leg on had slipped over my knee and I fell to the ground. I didn't hurt myself but I did feel a fool. Here I was lying on the pavement with the artificial leg hanging from my trouser bottoms. A bus was now parked opposite and a lot of people were staring at me and couldn't believe what they were seeing. For all the world it looked as though my leg had disengaged from my body or I just happened to have one leg about five feet long. Sylvia, seeing my predicament but knowing that I was ok, held on to a lamp post, beside herself with laughter. This set us all off in hysterics. With a little difficulty I managed to somehow restrap the leg though I was in some discomfort. It wasn't for long, however, another bus soon arrived and within minutes we were back at Sue's, still laughing, eager to tell the tale.

Over the years the same deep longing kept returning. I wanted to visit the graves of my fellow crew members, and the village where I had crashed to thank those who had helped to save my life.

Most Monday evenings Sylvia and I used to visit my sister Gladys where, by arrangement, we also met with Ruby and Reg. Once there were six of us, Ruby and Reg, Gladys and her husband Ken, and Sylvia and myself. We all had many similar interests and could argue without falling out. When Ken died I felt it very deeply and I miss him a lot. Now we are five, and our Glad, as I call her, has become even more special to us.

On one of these visits in 1982 someone mentioned an organised cheap weekend trip to Paris. We started to discuss the possibility of my longing being realised. Ruby said she would contact the Ministry of Defence. This she did and was given details of the cemetery and the location of the crash – Méligny-le-Grand, near Commercy, close to Nancy on the Paris Strasbourg Highway.

Bookings were made and Sylvia's sister Irene and Maria decided to come with us. Maria had taken an 'A' level in French and we wanted her to translate for us. Passports were not required as the coach operator had a special license.

When we started the journey I was very tense and, for no apparent reason, very irritable. The coach was quite comfortable and we reached Dover in about three hours. Fortunately the crossing was calm because neither Sylvia nor I were looking forward to this part. Most of the travelling was by night and we were quite tired when we reached the four star hotel. I have never been able to understand how these tour operators make a profit when you evaluate the cost against what they provide.

RAF Cemetery at Cholloy

Instead of going on the organised trip round Paris the next day we arranged to visit the cemetery, about thirty miles from Méligny-le-Grand. It was near a town called Toule on the main Paris–Nancy Rail Line. We had to have two taxis from the hotel. I was becoming more irritated because the time was passing so quickly and I knew in my heart we might not achieve my two goals of visiting both places.

The train was a luxury express and we passed Toule on the way to Nancy where we alighted. Maria was able to communicate with the locals and we quickly made our way to a bus stop. It was midday and we were still at Toule. The cemetery was approximately three miles away and we arrived there at 1500. I remember looking at the visitors' book and standing near the immaculate graves of my Crew. Rows and rows of neat well tended graves with their crosses showing Name, Rank and Ages. My daughter Maria cried, tears running down her cheeks, "Oh Dad," she said "I didn't realise everyone was so young," most being still in their teens. What a bloody waste, I thought – not just with our boys, but even when I saw the German cemeteries later.

The taxi driver waited for us and drove us back to Toule station. As I feared we didn't have time to go to Méligny-le-Grand.

We managed to catch a train back to Paris from Toule and, after waiting two and a half hours in a suburb, we arrived back at the hotel just before midnight. Everyone seemed edgy and nervous and my stomach felt as though it was knotted. I felt so miserable and depressed. I should have realised that this was how it would affect me.

I was so glad, however, that I had at last visited my Crew's graves. The visit to Méligny-le-Grand would have to wait but I was still determined to achieve this second goal.

13

The Return to Méligny

February 1986. It was now four years after my visit to the graves and I had been able to take early retirement. My thoughts were still of Méligny-le-Grand. Reg, who the previous year had driven through most of Europe on a holiday with Ruby and Gladys, said, "Come on, let's make arrangements to find this village where you crashed, we can all go in my car."

By this time Sylvia and I had our passports and we all started to get excited as plans were made. Within two weeks Ruby and Reg confirmed the date of departure – Sunday June 15. The following weeks seemed like an eternity. I could not wait as I was so impatient and excited.

Sunday, 15th June, 1986 – Sylvia and I had hardly slept as we were both excited and were up well before the alarm went off. We drank a cup of tea and before half past six had collected Gladys. Within half an hour my car was parked on Reg's drive and we were all on our way.

I sat in the front with Reg driving, the three ladies sitting in the back. Being a small car, a Peugeot 205, we expected a certain amount of discomfort for the rear passengers so it was agreed we would interchange. The ladies didn't seem to notice the discomfort, however, for when I kept asking to change over they all said they were comfortable. By half past eight about ninety minutes after we started Reg pulled into Toddington Service Station on the M1. Not many people can be as fortunate as I am in having a brother-in-law like Reg. He quickly made us cups of tea and we were all given our own packet of egg, bacon and sausage sandwiches he had prepared. We made good time through London but met long delays on the A2 London to Dover Road due to road works. Try as he might Reg couldn't make the midday ferry he had booked. Never mind. This gave us a chance to stretch our legs and eat the lunch that Reg had once again packed for us. It also meant the car was first on and off the next ferry.

The channel was as calm as a duck pond, the sun shining with no haze. There weren't many passengers on board and this made it easy to purchase whisky, gin and brandy from the duty free shop and to sit together afterwards. On the way over we put our watches back one hour to match French time. Customs called us through and by 3 o'clock we were on the motorway from Calais and heading for the "Hotel International" at St. Quentin. The sun was still shining when we pulled into a picnic area at the side of the motorway. I know the French charge for using motorways but this does mean less traffic and well maintained service areas. We finished off the large lunches and drank freshly made tea.

At six o'clock we booked in at the hotel and arranged to meet in the lounge an hour afterwards. This gave us a chance to change, rest and bathe. It was a lovely evening as we walked round this very clean town. Musical chimes rang from the Town Hall Clock as we meandered round the Market Square. A chip van was doing business in the square and the smell was so nice we decided to try some 'Frites' as the French call them. I can assure you they were delicious and we have tasted them many times since.

The ladies went walk about looking at the many shops. Reg decided to keep me company while I rested in the main square, being a little leg weary. To end a most pleasant day we sat over a drink and the ladies chatted whilst Reg and I switched on the TV and watched a World Cup Game before Sylvia and I retired.

Monday, 16 June – on the way to breakfast we met another English couple returning from holiday. I suppose they were in their mid 40's. The story the wife told revealed another aspect of war. Apparently her father was billeted with a French family during the War so she and her husband decided to take a holiday and visit them. Whilst there she was introduced to one of the daughters. She said it was like looking into a mirror and seeing herself!

After our continental breakfast we went for a walk round the open market. The sun was still with us and I began to wonder if this was just a dream. We didn't buy anything but admired the size of the fruit and vegetables on offer. I wondered if this would be the day when I would find Méligny-le-Grand and my rescuers. We drove for about two hours and stopped when we saw a roadside inn with chairs and tables outside. Driving in the sun had made us all a little uncomfortable and thirsty. Ruby and Sylvia joined Reg and I drinking the ice cold Stella Artois Beer which was so refreshing whilst Gladys drank coffee – very French.

Some kilometres on we had to go through Reims, a most beautiful city with its magnificent cathedral standing out in the sun on the skyline. I later learned it had been restored after the First World War. We followed the river Aisne right through the city centre, and seeing the barges berthed at the side reminded me of my youth. Sometimes I used to travel on similar barges in Birmingham that used to deliver all kinds of goods to the Black Country. How times have changed! Here in Reims the river is so wide the barges are almost big enough to sail the seas. I think in a way I was envious – it was the kind of life I could have enjoyed.

We bought bread, cheese, cooked ham, and a couple of bottles of wine, filled up with petrol and looked for a suitable spot to eat our lunch. This we did at the shady side of a wood near the main road to Toule.

We were now on our last lap and I was angry with myself at finding I had forgotten my copy of the French Ordinance Map which clearly showed Méligny-le-Grand. I had visited the library back home and obtained a photocopy of the area. I knew we must be close but I was a little concerned that we were travelling on a recently constructed road and I thought it might by-pass the village. We thought our luck was in when we spotted a police road check on the other side of the dual carriageway. I quickly made my way to one of the two gendarmes standing by a lorry. I showed him Reg's map and said "Méligny-le-Grand." The trouble was I was saying it phonetically and not as pronounced by the French. We could not communicate and I felt downhearted at this apparent set-back.

The time was now nearing 3 o'clock and Reg had driven longer than agreed. He had spotted a board advertising a hotel at Stainsville a few miles further back. We were there within minutes and afterwards all agreed this had turned out for the best. The hotel was a Chateau and full of character. We were able to make the lady owner understand we wished to stay the night and were led to large bedrooms with recently re-fitted bathrooms. After settling in the others went for a walk while I admired the hotel and grounds. I sat for a while and when the others returned we had tea in the garden. Later we met the male proprietor who could speak reasonably good English and promised to try and locate Méligny-le-Grand for us. This he did soon afterwards saying it was near to Commercy only twenty miles away. At this good news our spirits were lifted and we arranged to have a dinner to be cooked by him. Whilst waiting we were invited to play French bowls with the two young sons. The meal was excellent and after downing a couple of glasses of wine we made our way to Reg and Ruby's room. As at St. Quentin we filled our glasses with our individual choices and we were soon quite merry again. Long after we had gone to bed we could hear the two young boys playing bowls. This amused rather than irritated us.

Tuesday, 17 June – we had a continental breakfast outside in the garden and after flasks were filled with hot water and the bill paid we set off. The sun was still with us and we were all getting very excited. Reg decided to go to Commercy and ask for directions. Commercy is about three miles off the main Paris-Nancy Road. We parked in the town centre near to the market square and when we got out of the car it was now dull and overcast. Taking Reg's map with me I approached a group of men who were chatting. One of them suddenly realised I was giving the wrong pronunciation and said "Ah, oui Méligny-le-Grand" and pointed to a spot on the map. Reg had noticed a sign showing the way to the hospital where I had first been treated, a place I hope to visit one day, but my priority was Méligny itself and especially its people. Getting into the car I felt very excited and could not get to the village quickly enough.

We made our way back to the main road and, at a certain point, Reg noticed we had passed a lane that looked promising. He turned the car around and, after we had travelled less than a mile, we came to a village and noticed two ladies talking over the garden hedge, typical of home. Getting out of the car I asked if they could speak English. They both smiled but shrugged their shoulders. When I mentioned Méligny-le-Grand one of them pointed down the road. After about half a mile we came to cross-roads and we were back on the main road. Reg was the first to notice the sign to – YES – 'Méligny-le-Grand'!

The irony was we must have been within two miles the previous day but we all agreed that the rest, meal and wine in Stainsville had done us a power of good, refreshing us for today's adventure. Driving down the narrow road I felt very strange. Was it the right village? Would anyone still be alive who remembered the crash? It was over 41 years ago.

Suddenly the village and church came into view.

This was the church of St. Evre whose bells I had heard and crawled towards in the snow after the crash. The village was in a valley surrounded on all sides by wooded hills. Reg stopped the car and without a word we all entered this ancient church. Sadly there was no one inside so I came outside hoping to meet someone from the village I could talk to. I met a van driver who I think was a telecommunications engineer. He could not speak English but when I asked, "Is there anyone here who can speak English?" he seemed to understand and led me to the house next to the church.

The Bell tower of St. Evre

As I was approaching this house I noticed an old woman standing in the doorway of another house close to the church. Imagine my surprise when I was later introduced to her and told that she was Mme. Bouchot – the woman who had given me the egg, cut off my flying boot and nursed me immediately after I was found.

When I reached the house next to the church I was greeted by a young woman in her early 20s who said she could speak a little English. However, when I told her I was in the RAF and my plane had crashed upon the hill during the War, I could see she didn't understand. Again I asked if anyone could speak English. She seemed very excited and gesticulated that she was fetching someone to look after her three children. Within seconds she was back with a lady I later found out was her mother-in-law Yvette.

We were beckoned to follow her to the very last house in the village (with a population of 62). It was raining but not heavily.

Mme Bouchot and family

I was taken to a side door and a woman appeared, the only person in the village who could speak English – her name was Colette. Her husband Guy was working in his garden. "Could you help me please? I was in a bomber that crashed near the village during the night of January 7/8, 1945. People from the village heard my cries for help and carried me to a house." Colette explained that she wasn't from the village but from Verdun. She had worked for the American forces and that is how she came to learn English. Her husband came from the village and was serving in the army in Germany in 1945. They had married after the War and decided to buy their

Ruby and Colette at the feast

house. Another woman approached and they spoke for some time. Colette translated that this woman had remembered the crash and said Colette's house was originally a farm where one of the two crashed airmen had been taken. Colette then spoke to her husband who got on his scooter and rode down towards the village. He came back shortly afterwards followed by a man in a tractor who looked so happy and excited.

Colette introduced us, "This is André Fromont – André was the man who helped carry you to safety. He was also the bell ringer."

I shall never forget the look on his face. We shook hands warmly and smiled. He looked at me and said he couldn't carry me now! I think he meant I was a lot heavier. By now we had all been introduced to one another and we were asked if we would like to see where the plane had crashed. "Yes, of course, please," was our reply.

André

We drove a little way up a hill, parked the cars, and André led us to a wooded area. He pointed to an opening where small beech trees were growing and I knew this was where the plane had crashed and where I had crawled towards safety that cold morning so many years before.

André told me he had heard me calling for help. As we spoke, and as if 'the gods' were aware of what was happening, one clap of thunder rolled overhead, not at all frightening but eerie. We were all emotional and Reg said, "What a thing, what a thing!" Everyone, including Colette and Guy, was now excited. We offered André a bottle of whisky and, as we were expressing our gratitude, he insisted we went to his house to meet his wife

Yvette (whom we had met earlier) and the rest of the family. There we were given home-made wine and savoury biscuits.

Whilst Colette was translating for us André left us and opened a door at the rear of the kitchen. He spoke to Colette and, looking at me, gave me a small aluminium cake or loaf tin. Colette said André had salvaged parts of the plane, and a friend who worked in a foundry had made three of these tins from the wreckage. André wanted me to have one as a souvenir. What could I say, how could anyone express their true feelings in that moment? André and I looked at each other, contentment and happiness showing on both our faces. I knew then that I had met a good true friend.

Afterwards Ruby said we could be brothers. We were about the same age, André was 62 and I was 61. We both had good heads of hair, though now both grey of course. He has sparkling eyes with an innocent cheeky look on his face. We exchanged addresses and I promised to write soon. "Please come again," they said, Colette inviting us to stay at her home.

As we were about to leave who should walk into the room accompanied by her three children but the kind young woman to whom I had first spoken? Her name was Yolaine, the wife of Jean Pierre, André's son. Just one of many lovely moments in this story.

On returning to England Reg had the idea of engraving the cake tin with details of the crash. This he did and on our next visit to Méligny André insisted on exchanging it for a second cake tin. Reg then decided to have the second tin engraved with the same details but in French and on our next visit they were exchanged again.

Reg, Yvette, André, Ron, Sylvia, Ruby and Gladys
outside André's house

14

Fulfilment

I had such mixed emotions. My mind was still full of our visit to Méligny, of the past, and of André and his family. Something was missing though – our stay had been too short. I had been afraid of staying too long thinking we might have overstayed our welcome. How wrong I was! Within days of returning home I wrote to André saying how I felt at meeting him and his family. I said I looked forward to visiting him again. My letter was answered very quickly by his daughter Catherine who was staying with her parents for a rest during her pregnancy. She was able to write in English we could understand. I hadn't yet met Catherine as she and Pascal her husband lived near Paris.

The letter was so moving. They wanted us to return and stay for a few days. This was the news I wanted to hear. I quickly rang Ruby, Reg and Gladys who, when I read the letter to them, were as excited as Sylvia and me. We arranged our usual Monday night at Gladys's and spent hours talking about André, Yvette and their family. We were so overjoyed. Weren't we lucky meeting Colette, the only person in the village who could speak English? She and Guy couldn't do enough to help us.

Reg thought it would be a nice gesture when we were there to invite André, Yvette and their family, together with Guy and Colette for a meal. Holidays were again arranged and I wrote asking Colette to tell André we would like to return on Saturday 27th September, also mentioning Reg's treat.

Colette answered my letter saying André and Yvette were looking forward to us returning. Having her phone number I gave her a surprise call – she was so thrilled and said everyone was very excited at our forthcoming return visit. Also the day after our arrival was the Village Feast. All the families, brothers, sisters, cousins and friends get together and have a special Feast. This was to be a meal and a holiday of a lifetime. Memories to treasure for all time.

Friday 26th September – arrived at long last. David, Gladys's son, insisted on taking his mother, Sylvia and me to Ruby and Reg's. By 0700 hrs we were all on our way – the sun was shining in the heavens as well as in my heart. No longer did I feel irritable but so contented, a wonderful feeling indeed. This feeling was, I am sure, one we all shared.

We arrived at Dover in good time. Good old Reg once again had made all the arrangements, food and ferry crossings. Once on board we bought whisky for presents and drinks for ourselves of course. The channel crossing was so calm with the sun following us. We were quickly through customs and on our way to Belgium! Belgium? Somehow we had taken the wrong road but this was soon rectified and we were quickly on the motorway we wanted.

Reg being the driver said he would like to drive as far as he felt able, hoping to make our overnight stop that much nearer to Méligny-le-Grand. I was map reading for Reg and we agreed to try and find a hotel at Chalons-sur-Marne. This would only leave us about a two hour drive the next day to reach Commercy. We parked opposite a hotel but they were unable to accommodate us. However, they kindly recommended another hotel just round the corner. This turned out to be very comfortable with a number of other English guests also staying there. As before, once we had settled in, out came the drinks and we all became very giggly. It had been a very happy day for us.

Saturday 27th September – continental breakfast for us all and flasks filled. With time to spare we walked round the market square. Lots of stalls were open and also an indoor food market. The sun was full in the sky once more – it does put the icing on the cake when the weather is good. We filled up with petrol and were on our way, arriving in Commercy just before midday. Reg and I waited outside a supermarket while the ladies went inside to purchase food for a picnic. Dead on noon the town hooter blared out loudly. We hadn't realised that everything stops for lunch in France. Staff approached the ladies to say the shop was now closing, but they kindly allowed them to quickly make their purchases. En route to Méligny-le-Grand we spotted a picnic sign which led to a clearing in Commercy Forest. It was so eerie, a beautiful day but no sound at all. In England, once in the countryside, the air is full of different types of bird song but not so in France where they do tend to eat birds as a delicacy.

Finishing our picnic we set off on the last lap. The time was 14.41 when we drove down the lane into Méligny. Upon seeing us a young man on a motor cycle turned round and rode quickly back to the village. We all said we thought he had been sent to look for us. Guy and Colette were outside their house as we arrived. We stopped, got out and embraced them. Within minutes André arrived on his tractor. No words can adequately express how happy I was to see him again. Though neither of us spoke I could see by his expression that he was as happy as I was.

We all then made our way to the spot where the Lancaster had crashed. For some time Guy had been searching the area and had gathered bits and pieces of the aircraft still strewn on the forest floor. Reg could hardly believe the good condition of some of these parts and asked if he could keep some as mementos – I was only too happy for him to have them. André left us to return to his family whilst the rest of us went back to Colette's for a drink and savoury biscuits and to collect Reg's car. We said our good-byes to Guy and Colette knowing we would see them for dinner later that evening. On arriving at André's we were met by his wife Yvette. It is a lovely feeling when, looking at someone's face, you can see they are pleased to see you. Yvette, very much like André, has an honest face with clear sparkling eyes. I had never been more contented.

Gladys was given a bedroom next to ours on the ground floor. Ruby and Reg were in a bedroom upstairs. After unpacking, changing and tidying ourselves up, we all met in the large dining room. It was a little strange not being able to converse but somehow we managed to communicate. André beckoned us to follow him and led us to a building opposite the house. He and his two sons used it as an office. This weekend it had been converted to a dining room with chairs and tables for about twenty five people.

At 1900 hrs Guy and Colette arrived and we all set off for Commercy where Colette had booked our evening meal. The company was wonderful with Colette, and André and Yvette's daughters-in-law Yolaine and Sophie, all doing their best to translate for us. I suppose I was disappointed that André's family was not complete as Catherine was unable to be with us.

We returned to the village just before midnight and most of us, not being night owls, went to bed almost immediately – I slept like a log.

Meeting at breakfast the next morning – Feast Day – we had tea and toast. Reg our chef continued to spoil us. Knowing a lot of work was still to be done by André and his family for the Feast our party discreetly went for a car ride. The morning was beautiful, the sun was out, and it was warm but not oppressive. Reg drove us round the lanes and we all admired the scenery – apple trees on both sides with fallen fruit at the base of nearly every tree. All the fields were cultivated and what struck me was that France, with about the same population as Britain but very much larger, didn't waste any land – nowhere were any parts of fields overgrown, they were tilled right to the road's edge.

After a while, believing we were not eating till evening, we stopped at a village and bought milk, butter, bread and cakes. How I regretted this later! I have always had a good appetite and there are not many foods I do not enjoy. We stopped at a clean lay-by off the main Paris-Nancy road about two miles from the village for a picnic before making our way back to Méligny. The time was now 1130 hrs and Sylvia, Ruby and I wanted to go to the church service at noon. Reg and

Gladys went for a walk. I must confess I have never really felt comfortable when going to church but here I felt at peace. We were introduced to André's sister Anne Marie, brother-in-law Jean and nephew Robert. Yvette and Catherine were in the choir and the service was an experience I shall always remember with pleasure. I felt I was part of the village congregation and so happy to be in the church whose bells over forty one years ago had led me to safety.

Reg and Gladys met us outside the church and we walked to André's house, a mere twenty metres away. Then, surprise surprise, everyone made their way to the Feast. How anyone could describe this meal of meals I don't know – but I will try. Before the meal, however, we all made our introductions. The Mayor of Commercy and his wife sat opposite Sylvia and I. He could speak perfect English. Here was a very intelligent man of the world. He was the headmaster of a school in Commercy and was in the French Resistance during the War. I felt honoured to meet him, particularly as he was a friend of André's.

* * * * *

The Feast

This was indeed a feast for a king. André, with his sons Jean Pierre and Jean Luc, had erected six trestle tables placing them side by side lengthways. Each person had three drinking glasses, and each table had bottles of wine and bowls of punch André had made. The punch was magnificent. Even Sylvia, nor normally a drinker, said how beautiful it was. I sat next to André who was on my right, with Sylvia on my left. Robert, André's nephew, sat next to the Mayor and his wife. Robert kept looking at Sylvia in a most quizzical way whilst conversing with the Mayor. After a while the Mayor looked at Sylvia and said that Christopher, another nephew, was wondering if she had seen the American TV Soap Opera "Falcon Crest." Sylvia answered "Yes." The Mayor smiled and said, "Christopher thinks you look like Angela Channing." This caused some amusement, particularly when after the meal he approached Sylvia and said "Goodnight Angela."

After the Feast and feeling as full in my stomach as I have ever done, everyone made their way to the forest. Most of us, including the children, were still searching and finding more bits of the crashed Lancaster bomber. The children were in excellent spirits bringing the pieces to me and speaking in French. They must have been puzzled by my ignorance, not being able to talk to them. I still felt strange somehow and I suppose deliberately shelved the unhappy memories of the crash. Time, as older people will tell you, does

Reg and André's sister at the Feast

89

heal the wounds even if the scars remain. For many years after the crash I had nightmares re-living it and feeling involved whenever there were serious air accidents. As the years passed, however, so did these bad nightmares. I do confess though that I have never been one to bottle up my emotions. Talking about them right from the start seemed to make them so much easier to accept.

Photographs of André and his family were taken by his daughter Catherine to whom we are indebted for her tireless efforts to translate enabling both families to converse. After about an hour we meandered back to the village where Jean Luc, André's son, led us to a house he had almost completed. I thought what a clever and good young man he must be. A cellar had been dug out to hold his central heating system. A garage was incorporated into the detached house that had full double glazing. The carved fitted doors and woodwork were beautifully finished. How proud André and Yvette must have been of their son!

Walking back I was still full and I didn't know how I could possibly eat anymore when the evening meal started, little more than two hours after the lunch! When we entered the Feast room again it was nice to see Guy and Colette there.

They had been hunting during the day but without success. Jean, André's brother-in-law, made us feel at home right away. He had an accordion and when he saw us enter he started to play "Roll Out The Barrel!" We all started to sing and everyone joined in the good humour. The table was fit for a king again. After a wonderful evening we bade everyone goodnight and retired to bed around midnight.

On waking I was still on cloud nine even though we were leaving later that morning. Instead of being sad I was elated. The sun was still shining. After breakfast many photographs were taken and Yvette presented me with a bunch of red roses. Reg presented a tin of toffees to Mme. Bouchot and she in return gave us a bottle of Mirabelle. We kissed good-bye until the next time and on the way out of the village stopped and said farewell to Guy and Colette. We left Méligny-le-Grand before lunch and sped on our way. This had surely been the holiday of a lifetime.

15

The Memorial

At a meeting early in 1990 at Méligny-le-Grand the Mayor, M. Henri Guérin, and his councillors agreed to place a dedication memorial plaque in the church of St. Evre as part of a memorial service which was to be held on 20th May.

TO THE GLORY OF GOD AND REMEMBRANCE OF OUR COMRADES WHO GAVE THEIR LIVES IN THE FIGHT FOR LIBERTY JAN. 8TH 1945.
F/O JAMES SCOTT, F/O KENNETH DARKE, F/O ROBERT DUNLOP, SGT. LESLIE KNAPMAN, SGT. JACK ELSON.
FOR OUR TOMORROW THEY GAVE THEIR TODAY.

TO THE PEOPLE OF MELIGNY LE GRAND WITH THEIR HELP AND COMFORT WE SURVIVED OUR GRATEFUL THANKS.
SGT. RON NEEDLE, SGT. HARRY STUNELL.
WE SHALL NEVER FORGET.

The Memorial Plaque

With the help of Ruby and Reg we went about making all the necessary arrangements. Letters were sent to the Air Ministry to try and locate relatives of the crew who had died. I also wrote to Charlie Chester's Sunday Soapbox programme broadcast from BBC Pebble Mill in Birmingham. I asked him to put out an appeal for relatives of those whose addresses could not be found. From this appeal a friend of Jim our Pilot called Dr. Tom J. Renouf, M.M. of Musselburgh, wrote to me giving the name and address of Nan, Jim's sister, who now lived in

Canada. The brother of Les Knapman our Flight Engineer, who lived on Hayling Island, also wrote to me. Due to his age and ill health he and his wife were unable to join us at the service. However, we made contact and still keep in touch. Guy the brother of Kenneth Darke our Navigator also contacted me to say that he would let his other brother Peter know. Regrettably we were unable to trace the relatives of Bob Dunlop our Bomb Aimer even though his sister came to visit Sylvia and I in 1946 but we have since lost contact. We have had no response either from the family of Jack Elson our Mid-Upper-Gunner who I believe lived with his step-father.

Mr. Des Richards, Secretary of our 106 Squadron Reunion Association, was contacted and kindly arranged for a member of the Association, Alan Strudwick, to carve the plaque for the occasion. Sadly Alan died just before the plaque was finished but a friend of Des was able to complete it. Fortunately Alan's widow Barbara was able to join us at the ceremony in Méligny.

We regarded this occasion to be sufficiently important to inform the Lord Mayor of Birmingham, Mr Fred Chapman. Although he was unable to attend he sent two goblets inscribed with the City of Birmingham's insignia to M. le Maire, Henri Guérin. I presented the goblets to him at the start of the ceremony and he asked me to hand a letter of thanks to The Lord Mayor of Birmingham.

A good friend of Ruby, Reg and I, Michael Dryden, offered to fix the plaque inside the entrance to the church. Prior to the service Michael, Reg and I escorted the plaque to Méligny on 17th April, and with the help of Jean Pierre, André and Yvette's eldest son, Michael fixed the plaque to everyone's satisfaction.

A ferry was booked for 17th May returning on 22nd May. Several letters were exchanged with M. Guérin and accommodation was to be provided by the villagers of Méligny. We decided to break the journey by staying at the Hotel Renard at Chalon-sur-Marne (now called Chalon Champagne) – a memorable occasion. We all piled in to a large room we had

TELEPHONE
021-235 2040/1/2

Our Ref : AS/ARC

30 March 1990

Mr. R. Needle,
20 Spiceland Road,
Northfield,
Birmingham,
B31 1NJ

Dear Mr. Needle,

The Lord Mayor has passed on to me your recent correspondence with him
regarding your attempts to find your former RAF crew.

The Lord Mayor is most interested to note that you will be attending a
dedication service in France on Sunday 20 May, and although it will not be
possible for he himself to join you at this service he would be delighted
to give you a gift which you might like to present on his behalf to the
Mayor of the appropriate town in France.

Perhaps you would be good enough to contact me and we can make an
appropriate arrangement.

Yours sincerely,

Anne Shore
Lord Mayor's Secretary

Letter from the Lord Mayor of Birmingham

booked where Reg organised a spontaneous buffet with produce bought from a local supermarket. Everyone ate, drank, chatted, and became merry!

The next morning was rather more sombre and, after girding our loins, we set off for Commercy about 12 miles away to pick up other members of the party who had travelled by train. Before long we arrived at Méligny and were escorted to the Council House (also the village school!) where we met M. Guérin the Mayor, his councillors and all the villagers.

We also met Francis Guenon who owns the Military Museum at Ligny-en-Barrois who had kindly made a memorial stone which was placed at the edge of the forest.

The church bells rang out as a poignant reminder to Harry and I of that fateful day and to call everyone to the Memorial Service. Harry and I reflected with gratitude to God and the villagers on how fortunate we were to have survived the crash – the five others had not been so lucky.

After the Service we were led into the old school building where a feast had been prepared. Food and drink seemed to keep on coming and, amidst the solemnity of the occasion, there were humorous moments that we look back on with affection. Maria, my youngest daughter, genuinely thought her command of the French language improved relative to the amount of alcohol imbibed! Who was I to argue? Maria was the only one who had studied French to A level. Joyce Quarrie, a close friend of Sue's, also attended the event and spoke good French – she and Maria had much fun acting as interpreters. Although my son Renny's French did not improve with his drinking, it certainly encouraged him to find a most interesting spot to sleep – amongst the gravestones behind the low church wall!

The hospitality of the villagers was quite overwhelming at times and very humbling. They opened their homes and hearts to us all and gave of their very best. My daughter Sue and her husband Aggy stayed at the home of M. and Mme. Bouchot. Their son Pascal earned a living by breeding geese and

Renny, Sue, Ron, Maria and Sylvia outside St. Evre

force-feeding them to produce pâté de foie gras. The whole family were very proud of their product. Having seen the geese being force-fed Sue and Aggy were presented with the pâté as a starter at the dinner table. This was difficult enough for city dwellers (though they both told me it was delicious) but then followed the main course – geese hearts! Once again it was a bit of a struggle but they force fed themselves as they didn't have the heart to refuse! Later on in the meal when the hosts discovered that Aggy had a degree in theology, Madeleine Bouchot decided it would be amusing to get Aggy and Sue to sample a variety of home-made liqueurs in order to test their religious convictions – could they get them sufficiently squiffy to end up joining 'Titty' their dog – under the table!

On nearly all our visits we called at the first bungalow in the village – the home of Colette, the first person we met on our very first visit to Méligny where she and her husband gave us aperitifs together with various tasty morsels. They became our special friends.

The morning of the return home was naturally filled with sadness saying goodbye to André, Yvette and the rest of the villagers. The sadness was however reduced when André and Yvette made us promise to return the following year. It was further reduced by the amount of kissing that went on – everybody had to kiss everybody at least three times! Imagine the number of combinations that were involved – I was beginning to think we could end up missing the ferry!

What a debt of gratitude we owe, and me especially, to Le Maire, André and Yvette, their family and all the villagers of Méligny-le-Grand. A very special moment in our visit came when André and Yvette presented us with a cake that he had made for us to eat on our journey, along with jars of set honey for each of us from his very own apiary. Last but not least we were all given a bottle of home-made Mirabelle, a potent alcohol made from their own Mirabelle plums.

I would also like to mention here that the following year, along with my grand-daughter Samantha, a further visit was made staying at André and Yvette's. During our stay Mama Claire, Yvette's mother, paid for us, together with André and Yvette, to go on a day trip on a luxury boat along the canal. After two hours we stopped at a village and, by arrangement, met two vans with everyone's meals aboard – that's what I call service!

Another day we were taken to a fish farm in order to catch our evening meal. I was quite delighted to catch three fish but I think they possibly gave themselves up! We all enjoyed this special feast. During the dessert I happened to mention that one of my favourite cakes was chocolate. Much to my surprise the following day André's sister Anne-Marie brought along a large chocolate gateaux she had made especially for me.

In the evening after dark Catherine's husband Pascal drove us to the surrounding forests where we 'hunted' for deer but with a torch and not a gun. Once again I want to say how exceptionally kind and considerate André, Yvette and their family have always been to Sylvia, me and our family.

16

Fifty Years On

After several more visits to Méligny-le-Grand we returned in 1995 when the whole world was celebrating 50 years since the end of World War II. My family and I decided to try and celebrate with our friends in Méligny who were only too happy to oblige. The agreed date of our return was to be 20th August. This time it was agreed that I would hire a minibus and we booked the Dover-Calais ferry for 1530 hrs on 18th August returning on 22nd August, as well as overnight stops to break up the journey. Michael Dryden agreed to drive the minibus accompanied by his wife Hilda and their youngest son Laurie. Also on board were Ruby, Reg, Gladys, Harry, Sylvia and myself. On the way we had arranged to pick up Renny, Sue and Aggy and their children Sally, Sophia and Stefanos – there were 16 of us in total.

On our arrival at Méligny we were met and ushered into the Council House. After a drink and a bite to eat we split up and went to our respective homes in the village. Later we once again visited the Cemetery at Toule to pay our respects to those whose lives had been lost. We also gathered at the forest where the Lancaster Bomber had crashed and the children were still able to find pieces of the wreckage after 50 years.

On the Sunday morning we attended a service at St. Evre church after which we congregated at the old schoolhouse (also the Council House) for the Feast. For some weeks beforehand Harry and I had prepared an address in French that I would deliver. Along with the address (set out below) we presented a painting by Harry entitled "Bonjour Méligny!" Even now I feel embarrassed because, as hard as I tried, I could not manage the French accent but I believe our French friends appreciated my efforts.

Bonjour Méligny!

"This painting, "Bonjour Méligny!" is presented to the village of Méligny-le-Grand in recognition of the services rendered to the two survivors of a Royal Air Force aircraft which crashed and caught fire in the forest on the hill above your village on the snow-swept night of 7th January 1945. Five other members of the crew lost their lives, and their names are recorded on the marble plaque inside your church.

The young aviator in the picture looks down from a bright summer sky in the year 1944. He has no name because he represents a cavalcade of a thousand faces.

He looks down at the broad landscapes – the rivers and the wooded hills. He sees the winding roads and small villages spread over the earth as far as the eye can see and he wonders why a neighbouring country could sink so low as to hold this nation of France in captivity.

"Ah!" the unknown aviator whispers to himself – "Bonjour Méligny! – do not despair, for some day you will inherit the earth which has been stolen from you!"

Having voiced these supposed sentiments he speeds onwards towards the East and into an alien region which will greet him with the most unimaginable volcanic fury.

He is a very young man. Not long out of school. No more than a boy. Yet he is a temporary warrior engaged in serious matters imposed upon him by conquering hordes – the invaders. French, Dutch and Belgian people held in unspeakable bondage by those in pursuit of some wild, impossible Hitlerite dream.

The perils of airborne conflict are well known to this nameless young man, but he frequently smiles in order to conceal his doubts and fears. Also he is painfully aware of the rapidly mounting losses of Bomber Command – 56,000 at the final count. Of these 995 are from his own 106 Squadron who, in common with the assembled might of other Squadrons, deployed between 20 and 24 aircraft each with a crew of seven men. They flew, sometimes by day but more often by night, through inhospitable darkness, appalling weather conditions, and fierce enemy opposition from ground or air defences.

Somehow the resolve of a bandit nation which held the rest of Europe in chains had to be broken. A doctrine – not permitted to succeed – but even the stoutest hearts or the strongest nerves were tested to the uttermost limits, and the demands imposed by the round-the-clock bombing offensive were severe in the extreme; they traversed the sky-lanes via a multitude of strategic routes above occupied territories – crushed democracies.

And so we, the luckless crew of the aircraft which crashed on the outer perimeter of your village, became additions to the statistical mountain of losses. We spent the night in open country in one of the fiercest snow-storms in living memory with no immediate signs of habitation. Our senses were scrambled but miraculously, at daybreak, the fates were to favour us two injured survivors when we heard the uplifting sound of the Angelus bell from your village church indicating hope! And then rescuers appeared. They had come to help the living and to mourn the dead. They provided shelter, comfort and hope. Such memories are imperishable.

100

We are here today, more than 50 years later, our lives extended beyond our dreams, and for such blessings we are here to pay homage to the village whose rescuers have come to be regarded as blood brothers and sisters. Also to pay tribute to the memory of our comrades who lost their lives on your tranquil soil. We are mindful as well of the great numbers of our compatriots who died in the most drastic and varied circumstances, all epitomised by this symbolic unknown aviator in the picture here presented to you all.

"Bonjour Méligny!" We love you all. People once held in bondage but whose hearts and spirits had always been free. Long live the spirit of Méligny. We thank you most sincerely and wish you well."

Your English brothers,
Ron Needle and Harry Stunell.
August 1995

Harry and I also presented the Mayor, André and Yvette, their family and others with a memento – an RAF remembrance plaque.

At the Feast I well remember the cakes that Francis and Marie Odile provided. Francis owns the special Military Museum in Ligny-en-Barrois and has also become our close friend. I am grateful to Francis for all he has done, not just for me but for all his hard work collecting bits of the crashed Lancaster and making a special place for them in his Museum. The day passed with plenty to drink – wine, Mirabelle, whisky and other beverages – and more food than we could possibly eat.

On our way home we reflected on the marvellous hospitality and kindness afforded to us by the villagers of Méligny. After a very long journey we all arrived home safely. I am now in my 82nd year but well remember how exhausted Harry and I felt at the end of each journey. Despite this I hope, God willing, to make another visit with Reg to see André, Yvette and our other friends in Méligny soon.

ANDRE'S STORY

Here is the story of André Fromont – exactly as he wrote it: -

January 1945 – Remembrance

André – the bell ringer!

*I*n the North East of France, Department of Meuse, situated in a hollow, here is a little village. This charming country is surrounded with meadows, fields and woods. People living in Lorrainese villages, especially in a parish, take care of a farm, vineyard and garden. Each family has a kitchen, a poultry yard with chickens, and ducks for their own use.

The name of this village – Méligny-le-Grand.

You will easily understand that the inhabitants become intimate; at that time one hundred and twenty persons are living in the village: really like a big family. The year is 1945. You know, it is the War and not reassuring at all, and we try to help one's self. For the moment, it is quiet. I am twenty years old. Usually at that time I should have to be at the front, but luckily, my class is not called up for service. Several young men are in this situation. Each Sunday after supper we play cards with my parents and this evening my grandfather was with us. When he went back to his home, around 2000 hrs (you can see the woods through his bedroom window) the room was illuminated by bullets exploding in the forest and he supposed that a plane has fallen down in the wood.

Today is January 7th, 1945. It was snowing about five inches. During the night the storm-snow came back and it was freezing. When I get up in the morning the snow has left off falling. Today is Monday.

The Angelus has just rung as every morning (I am the bell-ringer). I go to carry out the milk to my Grandfather, living alone (daily action). He tells me that maybe a plane could be fallen not too far away because he heard the noise made by bullets exploding and he saw lights and sparks during the night.

Going out of his home I meet my cousin Albert, we are both the same age. I ask him if he heard any noise. But the storm was so loud that we couldn't hear anything. We decided to take a walk to the plane. Going out of the village Albert's father, who is my uncle, told us, "don't go this way." Answering him, we hear beside the woods, a voice. We decided to walk to this voice. However, we go to get assistance, because we are afraid; maybe a German plane crashed into the forest and they could shoot at us. We take a stretcher. Somebody takes a 'Mirabelle' pocket flask, (Mirabelle is an alcohol, 50%, distilled in the village).

Finally we arrive at this grove. We see a young man leaning back against a small tree. He is wounded; he makes us a sign with hands "comrade," doubtful as to us, he thinks we are German. Much to our surprise, he is really a friend, an Englishman (unfortunately, we do not understand at all when he speaks). He is very cold and shivering. I give him my velvet mufflers manufactured by my mother (during the War, we cannot find any clothes), then we give him Mirabelle to get him warm. M. Bouchot tells us: "not too much, he could be sick." We lay him on the stretcher and we go back to the village. How heavy is he, my shoulders are sore. It is not easy to walk on the snow. Finally, we arrive at our destination. M. André Bouchot (deputy-mayor) decides to take him home.

His wife welcomes him and cut his boot; his foot hurt him. She cooks a boiled egg for him.

Meanwhile, Albert and I decide to return to the grove; maybe we could find the plane if we follow in the footsteps of wounded. So we are going again to the grove, following a large mark on the snow. This mark is leading us directly to the plane.

What a sight! It is horrible! There are no words to express what we are feeling. The cockpit is still there. The wings are divided into sections. We don't have any chance to find a survivor. We see only mangled corpses. What a shocking nightmare! The only thing we have to do is to turn back.

When we arrive at the village, Albert and I relate what we have seen. We were told that another person stayed overnight within the sheep-fold located at the extremity of the village. When the airman heard the bells ringing, he came down to the watering-place and is rescued by M. Giroux who takes the horses to water. This young man is wounded and burnt. He had a narrow escape. Burns stop down to the waist where he carries a medal. M. Giroux takes him home.

The day before, his wife lent to a neighbour a warming-pan to warm up a bed. As soon as she saw this young man wounded and chilled to the bones she decides to lay him down on a bed. But she must get back this warming-pan being of use for this period. It is the only way to warm up the beds. In winter, it is very cold and bedrooms are not warmed.

We know that Englishmen take refuge in Sauix-En-Barrois, about three miles away. Do they know what has happened at Méligny? Anyway, they come to take them to the nearest hospital. At Commercy, the Military Hospital is managed by a competent surgeon. His name is M. Grumillier and we hope, with good medical care, these young men will recover a good health.

Before starting for Commercy, M. Bouchot put his address in the pocket of the first man rescued. Maybe in the future, they could send news of themselves.

Years have passed away and we did not get any news. What has happened? What has become of these young men? Are they got out of difficulties? Did they lose the address? They were not in a good physical shape and perhaps they forgot everything?

In and around the village many people comment upon the crashed plane. A friend of mine, living at Naives-En-Blois, Jean (now my brother-in-law), with his friend riding a bicycle to the next village to play accordion, (we have only this amusement) heard a plane flying above. It made a queer noise. He told to his friend: "Listen, it will not be able to go too far." "It looks like only one engine is available." The snow-storm was terrible and to ride bicycles being impossible, they went back home. Many people went to see the site of the air crash out of curiosity. Many people appropriated parts from the plane (don't forget, it's the War and we have nothing). Jean took a wheel and made a watering-trough for his animals. A woman picked up a smaller one to make up a wheelbarrow. As for me, I picked up some aluminium parts from the cockpit. I have a good friend working in a foundry and he made for me three cake tins.

I get married five years later. Now I have three children and when I look at these tins, often used, I have explained to my children they are coming from this tragical story.

I keep always these facts in my mind. A few metres further, the plane was on the other hillside and no one could hear the noise. The two survivors went to Méligny, because the bells were ringing and not hearing bells, they might not have been saved. Then, in such a case, why not to believe in miracles? And much to my surprise, forty-one years later, to meet again Mr Ron coming to see the place of the accident and to know if he could find anybody to remind him about these tragical hours spent under the stars. Yes! I am still here ...!

André Fromont

André, Ron, Syvia and Yvette
in front of the Memorial Plaque

HARRY'S STORY

"The Call Of The Angelus Bell"

This is a testimony of devotion to the villagers of Méligny-le-Grand and in memory of lost comrades.

These words are recorded to mark a series of remarkable events that occurred in and around your village at a time when mankind – although walking in darkness, still pursued the light which rekindles and enriches the human spirit. Such light can be manifested in a number of ways. By words, by deeds or by love – or even by agencies beyond our understanding.

Let us therefore attempt to explain the strands of such powers by commencing this long overdue narrative which began on the fierce snow-swept night of 7th January 1945. A stricken, low-flying RAF Lancaster aircraft, homeward-bound, faltered through your neighbourhood skies. It was on a gradually descending flight path, wounded from earlier events. Unknown to its occupants, the altimeter was registering incorrectly due to a number of causes including blizzard conditions. Tragically, it was soon to make violent contact with the snow-bound earth. Its flight had commenced many hours previously in Lincolnshire, England, but was destined to end on a wooded hill overlooking your village which nestles in a hollow formed by the surrounding hills.

When the plane crashed it was quickly transformed into a raging inferno. Five crew members died either from impact or fire, or both. Two young men somehow survived. Both were grievously injured and after separately releasing themselves, each thinking himself to be the sole survivor, crawled away to differing locations, alone with their fears of finding a place of safe refuge and assistance.

Harry's refuge

They peered through the driving snow at a landscape beyond the wood that looked featureless, bleak, uninhabited and inhospitable. There was no evidence of your village and they were confronted with a freezing, trackless wasteland with no visible markings to follow and remember, it was a dark mid-winter night.

The radio operator, aged 21, badly burned and devoid of clothing from the waist down, after much frantic wandering located an isolated sheep-fold. He collapsed into its interior. The small community of sheep viewed him nervously as the blizzard continued to rage about them.

The Rear Gunner, aged 19, badly injured with broken bones, internal impact injuries and frostbite, was rendered almost completely immobile. Yet he made slow, dogged and painful progress beyond the fringe of the wood. He had put only a short distance between himself and the wrecked aircraft in the most appalling conditions man is sometimes called upon to endure. The night was long, cold and cruel and these men seemed destined to perish from intense cold or from their injuries.

108

Daybreak,
8ᵗʰ January 1945

Light of day, as always in mid-winter, arrived agonisingly late. The snow-fall had reduced to mere flurries of scattered flakes. Mercifully too, the wind had dropped to a low murmur. However the choice of which way to go had still to be considered by each of the young men from their separate locations. The wrong choice of direction was certain to result in a very lonely death.

The Bell Tower of St. Evre

But then, as they pondered their fate, a most remarkable stroke of luck occurred. Or was it luck? They imagined that they could hear the faint ringing of bells. Was this to be the final great breath of hope that they were seeking? Was it the sound of bells or was it just half-crazed imagination?

Yes – without doubt, it was the sound of a bell, the "breath of hope" – launched into the bosom of the now becalmed wind, but from what agency did it come? What was its source, its origin? The wind carried its sound most favourably.

Please reflect briefly upon the following from the Gospel of St. John chapter 3 verse 8 that are central to the story:

"The wind blows where it wills,
and you hear the sound of it,
but you do not know where it is coming from
or where it is going."

The two men did not know where the sound was coming from. The bell-ringer knew not where the sound was going to! And so, on this fateful day, the commonplace, ordinary ringing of the Angelus bell of Méligny-le-Grand was transformed into the extra-ordinary.

It is worth explaining here what the Angelus actually is:-

The **ANGELUS** is a prayer recited by Roman Catholics morning, noon and evening. It provides an opportunity to pause in prayer and to contemplate the coming of God among men. It commemorates the Annunciation – The Angel Gabriel's announcement of the Incarnation to the Virgin Mary (see the Gospel of Luke 1 v26-38), and is punctuated by the ringing of a bell (see appendix).

Medieval Latin: "Angelus Domini" – "The Angel of the Lord".

> *Thus are the origins of the Angelus bell that alerted the two survivors who answered its beckoning call.*
>
> *The badly broken man, whose name is Ronald, had made pitifully small progress when he was rescued in response to his cries for help by a seeking rescue party who had learned of the crash.*
>
> *The bell-ringer, André Fromont, aged 20, helped carry the stretcher in company with others.*
>
> *Ron was carried through the deep snows to the house of the deputy mayor – André Bouchot. He had found safe harbour at last.*
>
> *The burned man, Harry, finally stumbled into the shelter of this very small village and received care and attention at the home of M. and Mme. Giroux.*

They were saved.

Harry Stunell

In Memoriam

I respectfully record the names of those who died and are buried at Toule in France, and while we will always remember them, I ask that special remembrance be made on the anniversary of their deaths when Masses are read for the repose of the souls of the departed.

The Crew's Graves at Toule

PILOT	FLYING OFFICER	JAMES SCOTT
NAVIGATOR	FLIGHT LIEUTENANT	KENNETH DARKE
BOMB AIMER	FLYING OFFICER	ROBERT DUNLOP
ENGINEER	SERGEANT	LESLIE KNAPMAN
MID-UPPER GUNNER	SERGEANT	JACK ELSON

May the Lord be with you all, and may we always listen to the Angelus bell with reverence and humble thanks.

Fraternally Yours,

Ronald Needle – Rear Gunner

Harry Stunell – Radio Operator

17

The Sacrifice

It is estimated that about 125,000 aircrew served in the squadrons and operational training and conversion units of Bomber Command during the Second World War. Approximately 73,000 became casualties of which 56,000 were fatalities. Since for the greater part of the War Air Gunners and Wireless Operators/Air Gunners made up about half of the crew of an aircraft, it is likely that losses attributable to this group could be in the region of 20-25,000.

106 Squadron operated on 496 nights and 46 days, flying 5,834 operational sorties. In so doing it lost 187 aircraft and 995 crew, but, in addition to the success of its missions, on the credit side its gunners claimed 20 enemy aircraft destroyed, 3 probably destroyed and 29 damaged. A total of 267 decorations were won by the Squadron, including a Victoria Cross awarded to Sergeant N. C. Jackson for conspicuous bravery during an attack on Schweinfurt on 26/27th April, 1944.

The last Mission Record of Lancaster PB724 is but a single testimony to the great sacrifice made by the air crews of Bomber Command. Although we do not understand why some are spared and some not we can only acknowledge that we are here for a season and such seasons vary in duration. The cut-short seasons are beyond our comprehension.

Human conflict is the work of man. Its results can be devastating and we become involved in its processes by exercising the free-will we have been given. However, it is comforting to note that interventions do occur when all seems lost. Such interventions manifested themselves at Méligny-le-Grand in January, 1945.

We know only a few of the names of those who came to the rescue of Harry and I on that fateful night, but we wish to offer our eternal thanks to all helpers-in-brotherhood, and generally to the people of the village and, of course, its church of St. Evre, and also to the undying spirit of France.

We shall always remember you.

The last Mission Record of Lancaster PB724

18

Final Reflections

My relationship with André, his family, the villagers and indeed Méligny-le-Grand itself, was now an important part of my life. After Christmas and early in the New Year we always think about those momentous days in January, 1945, and of returning to Méligny-le-Grand. On one occasion during our journey there I was feeling sad – "had we worn out our welcome, would they be fed up with us?" I needn't have worried for on arriving at André's house the welcome was, and always has been, one of gladness to see us. We would visit Jean Pierre's and Jean Luc's houses where a special meal would be prepared. It was as if it was our first visit the welcome was so warm and inviting.

We always seemed to have the time to visit Anne Marie and Jean André's sister and brother-in-law who lived about four miles away. They had a farm with both produce and cattle. The steaks we had for our meal were out of his world! In the winter Jean, his children and Jean Luc who worked for Jean, would make wooden products for sale.

As well as the extraordinary clap of thunder that accompanied our first visit to the forest at Méligny there was another remarkable event that we often reflect on. On one of our early visits to the graves of the crew at Cholloy near Toule, about 10 to 12 miles away, André, Reg and I realised we were lost as the cemetery is a difficult place to locate.

We tried a number of new routes and became concerned that we might not find it until, driving along one road I had never been on before, I suddenly said, "It's here." Lo and behold within yards we reached a T junction and facing us was the cemetery! What made me say or know that the cemetery was so close to us is a mystery.

As the years passed I was losing family members. Apart from Elsie we lost Ted and then Gordon. I was the oldest survivor and truly thought "it's my turn next." How guilty I felt when next we lost Dennis, Don and lately Ruby. In the past two years Sylvia has battled bravely with many ailments, not to mention a double hip replacement, but all these things could not prevent her from attending her grand-daughter Sally's wedding to Richard Mayers in February 2005. Despite all she continues to cope admirably.

More than ever these things have made me think, "Live each day as if it is our last because one day it will be." I felt this even more so when we lost our son Renny.

There are good days and bad days in most people's lives. One of the nicest parts of 2005 was when Maria and Sue arranged a party for our Diamond Wedding Anniversary. We invited family and friends old and new. It was good to see friends from our younger days once again as well as from both our workplaces. Over 100 came. How proud we are of both our girls – how much we love and admire them! The party wasn't a modern disco affair; instead the stage had been prepared to resemble a World War II air raid shelter – sandbags and all. I almost hid under the table when sirens went off! It was great fun and everyone enjoyed the evening. As we feasted on piping hot beef, pork, salmon, hot potatoes and all the trimmings we also delighted in many famous "Songs that won the War" from the 40s and 50s as well as looking at a selection of photographs of family and friends down through the years projected on a large screen. Unknown to Sylvia and I, however, our daughter Maria had written to Buckingham Palace resulting in us receiving a card from Her Majesty the Queen congratulating us on our Diamond Wedding Anniversary. Maria also telephoned the "Birmingham Evening Mail" who sent a photographer to our home to take photographs of Sylvia and I as well as well as using our wedding photograph. The story and photographs appeared in the newspaper on our Anniversary date, November 24th 2005.

I would like to end my story by giving details of a greetings card sent to us by an unknown person. The envelope containing the card showed our address minus the number of the house. At the bottom of the envelope was written "I'm sorry Post, have not got the number but hope you can help"! The postman certainly did help and was able to deliver the card:

Just a few lines to congratulate you both on your recent Diamond Wedding. (Bham Mail).
Good luck to you both.
Without your courage and dedication (all of you) during WW2 we would not be free today.
We must never forget what you did for our freedom
Have a Happy Christmas
Best wishes for the New Year
Many thanks from a local person born in Northfield

To Mr + Mrs Needle and Family

Hope today is just the beginning of another happy year for you.

I do hope that when this story of mine is published this unknown person will read it.

My thanks to all and may your God go with you.

Appendix
THE ANGELUS

Priest: The angel of the Lord brought tidings to Mary :
All: And she conceived by the Holy Ghost.

Priest: Hail Mary, full of grace, the Lord is with thee; blessed art thou among women, and blessed is the fruit of thy womb Jesus.

Bell rings
3 times

All: Holy Mary, Mother of God, pray for us sinners, now, and at the hour of our death. Amen.

Priest: Behold the handmaid of the Lord :
All: Be it unto me according to thy word.

Priest: Hail Mary, full of grace, the Lord is with thee; blessed art thou among women, and blessed is the fruit of thy womb Jesus.

Bell rings
3 times

All: Holy Mary, Mother of God, pray for us sinners, now, and at the hour of our death. Amen.

Priest: And the Word was made flesh :
All: And dwelt among us.

Priest: Hail Mary, full of grace, the Lord is with thee; blessed art thou among women, and blessed is the fruit of thy womb Jesus.

Bell rings
3 times

All: Holy Mary, Mother of God, pray for us sinners, now, and at the hour of our death. Amen.

Priest: Pray for us, holy Mother of God :
All: That we may be made worthy of the promises of Christ.

Priest: We beseech thee, O Lord, pour thy grace into our hearts; that as we have known the incarnation of thy Son Jesus Christ by the message of an angel, so by his cross and passion we may be brought to the glory of his resurrection. Through Jesus Christ our Lord.

Bell rings
9 times

All: Amen.